How to Speak
So Others Listen

Maryam Pasha is a storytelling strategist, producer and curator. She is co-founder of XEQUALS Studio, a creative studio dedicated to telling stories across live events, film and theatre that create a just, sustainable and joyful future. She is a Director and Curator for TEDxLondon and TEDxLondonWomen and supports TED's climate initiative, Countdown.

As a storyteller and coach she has worked with hundreds of speakers, including philanthropists, Nobel-prize-winning academics, business leaders, technical experts, activists and students. She has helped organisations to raise over $1.5 billion to fight climate change, worked on talks that have been viewed over 25 million times and supported activists who've successfully changed the law in England to protect girls from child marriage.

Maryam co-hosts the *Climate Curious* podcast with Ben Hurst, which has recently passed 4.5 million downloads in just over 5 years. Her new podcast *Screw this . . . let's try something else* with Matt Golding, tells the stories of ordinary people all around the UK who are coming together to make their areas, and our systems, work better for everyone.

She is an advisor for Climate Spring, a visiting Fellow at Oxford University and a new mum.

How to Speak So Others Listen

Use Storytelling to Become a Better Public Speaker

Maryam Pasha

Copyright © Maryam Pasha 2026

The right of Maryam Pasha to be identified as the Author of the Work has been asserted by her in accordance with the Copyright, Designs and Patents Act 1988.

First published in 2026 by Headline Home
An imprint of Headline Publishing Group Limited

1

Apart from any use permitted under UK copyright law, this publication may only be reproduced, stored, or transmitted, in any form, or by any means, with prior permission in writing of the publishers or, in the case of reprographic production, in accordance with the terms of licences issued by the Copyright Licensing Agency.

Cataloguing in Publication Data is available from the British Library

Trade Paperback ISBN 9781035430338
ebook ISBN 9781035430314

Typeset in 14/18.5pt Dante MT Std by Six Red Marbles UK, Thetford, Norfolk

Printed and bound in Great Britain by Clays Ltd, Elcograf S.p.A.

Headline's policy is to use papers that are natural, renewable and recyclable products and made from wood grown in well-managed forests and other controlled sources. The logging and manufacturing processes are expected to conform to the environmental regulations of the country of origin.

Headline Publishing Group Limited
An Hachette UK Company
Carmelite House
50 Victoria Embankment
London EC4Y 0DZ

The authorized representative in the EEA is Hachette Ireland,
8 Castlecourt Centre, Dublin 15, D15 XTP3, Ireland (email: info@hbgi.ie)

www.headline.co.uk
www.hachette.co.uk

For Nima,
may you grow up in a world shaped by better stories

Contents

Introduction 1
Three steps to giving a great talk
    (or how this book is organised) 12

Section 1
Planning

Why planning is important (but often overlooked) 19
1. What is your big idea? 22
2. Who are you talking to? 31
3. Why should they care? 41
4. What are your key ingredients? 49
5. What is your unique perspective? 55

Section 2
Assembly

Why storytelling is so effective 63
How to begin 73
    Amplification: change the scale 75
    Sensory: bring it to life 78

Personalisation: make it relevant	81
False Start: surprise them	84
Puzzle: make them think	87
Question: make them wonder	89
Narrative: tell a story	93
How to choose?	96
How to structure your story	99
Story Sandwich	102
Problem-Solution	105
The Hero's Journey	109
The Heroine's Journey	112
Kishotenketsu	114
Pixar Pitch	117
The Mountain Range	120
In Medias Res	123
Sparklines	126
Nested Loops	129
Structures to consider when more than one person is presenting	131
Petal structure	131
Converging Ideas	132
Deciding on the right approach	134
How to use analogy and metaphor	135
How to wrap things up	140
Call To Action	141
Take A Stand (with me)	144
Zoom Out	146

Callback	148
Reframe with a twist	150

Section 3
Delivery

Why delivery matters (after you've done everything else)	155
Finding your authentic voice	158
What to do with your hands (and other things)	166
How (not) to memorise your talk	176
Avoiding death (or boredom) by PowerPoint	187
Getting useful feedback	193
Why I don't believe in 'Impostor Syndrome'	201

Section 4
Common Questions Answered

Do I need to do anything differently when I speak online?	213
My boss has asked me to start presenting at work and I don't want to mess it up. Help!	217
I've never done public speaking before and I'm really nervous. How do I get over it?	222
Can I really change the world with a story?	231
How do I tell a difficult personal story?	237
How do I prepare for a TED or TEDx talk?	241

I've been asked to chair a panel and I'm nervous! How do I prepare?	246
I've been asked to give a speech at a wedding! Help!	251
How can I use public speaking and storytelling to be better at networking?	254
Can I use storytelling when I'm trying to fundraise?	257

What Now?

How to use your time effectively (or my theory of quadrants)	263
Why we need your voice	269

Further Resources	273
Watch	275
Read	277
Listen	277
Acknowledgements	279
Index	281

Introduction

Public speaking is not just for other people. Public speaking is for you.

There is nothing fundamental that sets you apart from the people you perceive as good public speakers, even great public speakers. I know this fact better than most. I help take some of the world's biggest, most challenging, complex and important ideas and transform them into high-impact stories for every kind of audience. I work with everyone from billionaire philanthropists and award-winning academics to business leaders and students. I've worked with expert speakers but also with people who have never done anything like this ever before.

Even now, it feels improbable that I'm a speaking coach: I am not one of those 'natural speakers' you might have convinced yourself exists. Sure, as a kid, I was a chatterbox. I loved talking to people and I loved asking questions. I grew up with my grandma telling me stories, and every night I'd marvel at her ability to weave together characters, comedy, intrigue and suspense. As I got older, my parents would let me sit with their friends as they got into heated political discussions, encouraging me to join in.

But I also remember being told, as a little girl, that I talked too much. I remember never fitting in at school, being bullied for years for being different – fat, poor, brown: take your pick. I remember being told I was a terrible writer by a classmate, after which I spent most of my life avoiding writing at all costs. As I slowly internalised all of this, my voice was silenced, my insecurities grew and I stopped speaking. I hoped that it might make me more likeable or at least less visible – less of a target.

Likewise, in my professional life, I spent years struggling to find my voice. I always felt either too loud and angry (and therefore too visible) or ignored and overlooked (and therefore not good enough). I remember gathering the courage to tell my boss about experiencing racism from a senior colleague just to be told 'Maryam, you have been taught to look for these things where it just doesn't exist.' I remember sharing ideas that were laughed at, until someone else suggested them – an experience many women can relate to.

With each incident I would shrink. I would hide my work, I would avoid sharing ideas and I would avoid all public speaking and all writing. I would just get on with it, accepting that I would probably be invisible for ever.

But I didn't get to where I am today by feigning confidence and pressing on until someone noticed. Opting to 'fake it til you make it' isn't a long-term solution, since it doesn't address the underlying reasons why you feel insecure. Contrary to what you may have been told, becoming a powerful public speaker doesn't start with confidence at all, and even the most experienced speakers can feel nervous or worried ahead of a speaking engagement.

When I founded TEDxEastEnd in 2011, I never imagined that supporting our speakers would become something I would do for a living. But over time I started to see how so many people I was working with were feeling the same way I was. Years later a friend of mine asked me to run a workshop for his team, and when I sat down and distilled everything I had learned from supporting TEDx speakers into a set of tools, it became obvious to me that, to become a great speaker, there are no shortcuts. There isn't a hidden secret or formula, and, likewise, there is not one singular way of being a 'good speaker'. We can all master public speaking through storytelling with time, effort and practice. Every time you speak, you can get just a little better than the time before.

I also realised I had become a storyteller.

I'll talk more about storytelling as we go on, but, for me, it's at the absolute core of how I approach public speaking. For me, great public speaking is great storytelling.

It starts with building your skills, because storytelling and public speaking, like everything, are skills that you can develop with time, practice, and a little bit of support.

If you picked up a book on public speaking forty years ago, it would have told you that public speaking is one of people's most common fears, and we haven't gotten any less scared of it since then. After working with hundreds of speakers, I can attest to the fact that most people don't enjoy it, nor do they think they're any good at it. But improving your relationship to public speaking will allow you to approach these situations with less anxiety, and one day you might even enjoy it.

Public speaking is not just something that happens on a stage, in front of a large audience, or at a podium in front of the press. For me, public speaking is about speaking with a purpose, and that can happen anywhere, anytime and with anyone. That could mean being introduced to new people at a party, or making a contribution in a meeting at work.

I have spent over ten years working with speakers, from CEOs and philanthropists to students and campaigners, and I want to share that knowledge with you. In this work, as well as in my capacity as the Director and Curator of TEDxLondon, and a curator for TED's climate initiative Countdown, I have supported hundreds of people to develop their ideas into compelling talks and presentations. My approach can be applied across all scenarios, from tiny, intimate settings to those classic 'public speaking' moments when you're alone on a stage in front of hundreds or thousands of people.

The techniques I will be sharing with you in this book are the same ones I use to coach these speakers (some of whom you'll also be hearing from). In some cases, those speakers' talks have gone on to reach millions of viewers, but it doesn't matter to me and shouldn't matter to you whether your audience is one person or millions. These techniques can help you influence and persuade in simple but effective ways.

'Simple but effective' is the mantra I want to apply throughout this book. My intention is to make this a practical resource, not abstract theory. I want it to be something you refer to in a moment of need, or simply when you need a reminder of how to optimise *your* opportunity for public speaking.

We are at a point in time where it's crucial that more people are able to speak more effectively and tell better stories that have greater impact. Why? Because the ideas that got us to the present cannot be the ideas that carry us into the future. It's vital that these new, radical ideas full of potential are presented in a way that people will listen to, but it's okay if you need some help getting them there.

Something I also want to address with this book, as someone with a marginalised identity, are the structural factors that might make you feel that you're not a natural-born public speaker. Who gets to speak? But even more than that, who gets to speak and be listened to? Who is perceived as an authority in their field? It makes sense: when you look at the examples of who is held up as being the best and most captivating speakers, they are mainly older white men – Steve Jobs, JFK, Churchill.

It is entirely natural that, if you come from a marginalised identity or if your appearance doesn't fit our cultural expectations of 'authority', you may have internalised messages that say your voice isn't worth listening to, isn't powerful, doesn't carry an important message. I actually spent time earlier in my career researching 'impostor syndrome', which I have since come to reject as a concept in favour of a more structural analysis of exclusion. I'll go into this in more detail later in the book, but a key element of *How To Speak So Others Listen* is acknowledging these structural factors rather than spinning them as personal insecurities.

There are so many reasons why any of us could feel voiceless, regardless of how knowledgeable we are. I worked with a brilliant scientist who felt she needed to emulate older male scholars to be taken seriously and so forfeited her flair for storytelling and her vulnerability. Contemporary feminist discourse often encourages women to 'communicate like men' in order to win the respect of a sexist society, taking out phrases that 'soften' emails or using language that leaves no room for doubt. But I can't help thinking that maybe what a harsh, divided, absolutist world sometimes needs is more doubt, more gentleness – and if that's your personal approach regardless of your gender, then it's unlikely you'll benefit from bending yourself to fit a different communication style.

There was a business leader I worked with who felt that his non-English accent meant that no one could understand him, so he wouldn't accept any speaking invitations. And then there's the young entrepreneur who didn't think her authentic voice was professional enough. There are so many stories of people I've come across who have found reasons to think they weren't good enough to speak. They are almost always, without fail, rooted in structural discrimination. I can't solve that, but I can, instead, reassure you that I've helped speakers navigate some of these things that were holding them back.

Confidence is only one piece of the puzzle. It would be inaccurate to say it's not a factor in becoming a good speaker, but it's certainly not the be all and end all. When you're in those situations, when you're being doubted, where assumptions are being made of you, where you have to overcome more than others might have to overcome, it's even more essential that your story and your storytelling and your speaking is airtight, because then it leaves no room for doubt.

This book isn't about giving you superficial and unproven tips and tricks on how to 'fake it' and look like a great speaker. Too often, we're told that public speaking is about style over substance. Those days, if they ever existed, are gone. Audiences today are savvy. There is great content available everywhere, and so your message is infinitely more important than anything superficial, like the style or your delivery.

What matters is what you say. In my experience, once you love what you are saying, you will start to build your confidence around it too, and that confidence will be built on a solid foundation. Throughout this book, I will take you through everything else you need. How to decide what you are going to say, how to build a narrative around your ideas and how to keep your audience listening. There are clear structures, formats and methods you can practise and perfect to be great at speaking – whether that be to one person or a whole auditorium.

Over the process of researching and writing this book, I spoke to lots of different people who I consider experts in their fields. One of these is Alana Drew, who's TEDxLondon's Head of People. She told me a story about how, as an eight year old, she loved public speaking and progressed through competitions to give prepared speeches. Everything was going well . . . until it wasn't. 'And then we had to do an impromptu speech. I remember it to this day. We got put in a classroom with all of the kids who were competing, and you had five minutes to write an impromptu speech about dreams, and then you had to go and deliver it to the entire school. I remember being in this room and just thinking, *I've got nothing.* All the other people were scrawling, and I've got nothing. So we went out, I got up on stage, my mum was there, and all I had was, *dreams are really good.* And I cried and I ran off stage because I was so overwhelmed.' Alana was someone who loved public speaking, but being thrown into a new context with no support and being expected to perform to the same standard completely knocked her confidence. I think this is the experience of a lot of people when it comes to public speaking: that if you're used to presenting in internal meetings, you're not necessarily feeling as confident about pitching for new business; and being a great one-to-one networker does not necessarily translate to delivering a TEDx talk. If you feel like you're being thrown into a new situation with no support or tools, I hope this book will be something of a toolkit for you.

In my work with hundreds of speakers over the years, I've found one particular approach has worked well across the board and I am using it as the basis for this book. This involves breaking the experience of public speaking up into three distinct phases: planning, assembly and delivery. Maybe you only need help with one of these, in which case feel free to just refer to that section. As I said, this is intended to be a practical resource that you can refer to whenever you need. But if the idea of public speaking intimidates you or you have a big event to prepare for, I hope that every section contains information you find useful and reassuring. I want you to leave this book with the feeling that you are a competent storyteller, and if you're not *yet*, then you will be with practice. It is not beyond your reach, it is not for other people – it is for you as much as anyone else. It might surprise you to learn that I actually think this book is equally useful for people who aren't beginners: those with a solid foundation in their field, who have done a bit of public speaking and feel like they want to level up, and learn skills and structures that will help them share their knowledge with more people in new and more effective ways.

All you really need are the practical tools and emotional confidence to get you through your speaking engagement, whether that's a job interview, a panel discussion, a conference, an end-of-term speech. Throughout the book I'll share thoughts and ideas from my colleagues and friends in different sectors from healthcare to activism, all of whom find themselves speaking about different things, for different reasons. These are often the stories of people who weren't 'born storytellers' or 'natural public speakers' but who learned how to become one in service of their unique message.

Although this book is not specifically about preparing you for giving a TED or TEDx talk, you'll find, as you read, that it is grounded in the three things that have made TED so successful: focus, storytelling and authenticity. All three of those things are totally possible for the person you are right now.

So, to recap, you're about to find out that:

1. Public speaking is a skill you can learn
2. We're going to be using storytelling to make your public speaking the most effective it can be
3. It's about your content, not style

4. And I'm going to help you structure that content for maximum impact
5. You don't have to sacrifice your authenticity to get people to listen to you

Whatever your reason for reading this, you have something to say, and I want you to be able to speak so others listen.

Three steps to giving a great talk (or how this book is organised)

Imagine trying to cook a Michelin-starred meal by taking everything out of your fridge, throwing it in a pan and heating it on the stove, and then being surprised when it turns out like a mess. You wouldn't do it, right? But, so often, when I'm working with people who have a public speaking engagement on the horizon, it feels like that's how they're trying to approach the task.

I am here to tell you that this doesn't make sense, and to help you find a better way. You can't get the end result you want by throwing everything you know at the wall in front of your audience and seeing what sticks.

The main part of this book is broken up into three sections: planning, assembly and delivery. All three of these phases of the process are vital, and you can't have one without the others. These steps are equally important and useful, whether you're speaking in a formal or informal context, to loads of people or only a handful.

To go back to our dinner analogy, if you want to make a great meal, you're probably going to follow a recipe. But which recipe? And, for that matter, have you even decided what you're going to make?! How many people do you need it to serve? Do any of them have allergies? So, clearly, first you need to know what you want the end result to be, and who you're serving it to. Then you can choose the recipe that will get you there. Say you decide the answer is to make mac and cheese (as it so often is!). There are thousands of recipes: which one are you following? Once you know that, you can go to the supermarket to shop for the ingredients for the mac and cheese you're going to make. Are you using wholegrain pasta or regular? How many kinds of cheese are you including? Breadcrumb topping? It's only once you've made all those decisions, navigated all of those different considerations, that you can come home with your bags of shopping and start actually cooking.

Of course, this book is not about cooking. It's about public speaking. But both require planning. Without a plan, you're just left with a bit of a mess. Planning is the foundation of everything: it's deciding what you're going to make, finding the right recipe to suit your guests, and shopping for the ingredients. Or, in our case, it's figuring out what your message is, who you're speaking to, and how to engage them.

Assembly is the cooking part: how you actually combine the ingredients you've decided on to create the most effective talk/story/pitch possible. Of course, that seems like the most important bit, but it should also be obvious that that phase is impossible to do well without doing the planning phase first!

Assembly is where most of the storytelling approach comes in, and although I have a whole section on the 'why' of storytelling coming up, I just wanted to take a moment to hype it up. Storytelling, for me, is where we create those emotional and psychological connections that make big changes possible. It's about going beyond facts and figures to find the human story, the sparks that ignite people's curiosity and desire to dig deeper and know more.

And, finally, I like to think of delivery as the plating up: it's everything you do to make it a gorgeous, photogenic feast for the eyes. But as I'm sure you know from many a disappointing meal, you can't rely on that alone. You can't fully enjoy a meal that looks great but tastes bad or bland, and you definitely can't eat a meal that you haven't even been able to cook because you didn't buy any of the ingredients! But that's not to diminish the importance of delivery. While you can't get by on looks alone, you can, conversely, plate something incredibly delicious in such a way that it puts people off eating it!

Now, if you were having a dinner party, you hopefully wouldn't choose to make three courses of extremely complicated and high-skilled dishes that you'd never made before. Same goes for this: I really recommend approaching one element of public speaking at a time and trying to master it specifically. Look for opportunities to hone those skills and divert your attention towards only that, instead of trying to do everything all at once. If you try to do everything right from the start, you'll probably get frustrated and give up, but I want to set you up for success. It will also be helpful to have a specific event or opportunity in mind as you read this book, so you can imagine how you'll apply your new knowledge and ideas in practice.

If you're new to public speaking and you want to get a handle on this stuff, the first thing to do is to set yourself up to feel as calm and in control as humanly possible. If you've been doing public speaking for twenty years, meanwhile, you're hopefully still going to find something here that'll help you be even better. A few people have ended up sitting in on my public speaking workshops two or three times, and the feedback I always get from them is that they take something new away every time. I really believe that this approach I'm sharing with you works, and contains all the elements you'll need to become a confident public speaker, using storytelling to your advantage.

It'll roughly look like this:

1. Planning – generating ideas, thinking about your audience
2. Assembly – using storytelling to inform structure and content
3. Delivery – bringing it to life in your unique way

After you've taken in those three sections, you'll be well equipped to speak so others listen.

Section 1
Planning

Why planning is important (but often overlooked)

How did you feel when you knew you had to put together a talk and do some public speaking soon? Excited? Nervous? Overwhelmed? All of the above? Regardless of how you're feeling, the one thing you're *not* going to do is open PowerPoint and try to figure out how much you can cram into your allotted time. Instead, you're going to step back and take a moment of calm. That's how I think of the planning phase: we're not actually *writing* anything at this point, but we *are* doing a lot of thinking. We're contemplating, we're ruminating, we're considering. Maybe that's what we all need a little bit more of.

I get it – most of the people I work with want to get *stuck in* and start hashing out the details as soon as they know they have to speak. Whether that means creating the slides or writing the content or even doing an outline, there's always an impulse to dive right in. And we will dive in, I promise, but first we plan.

For me, the planning phase is essential. Without it, you sometimes end up with a beautifully crafted speech that follows a wonderful narrative trajectory, all before realising . . . this isn't actually making the point that I want to be making, in this moment, to these people. The planning phase is about making sure that all the key ingredients line up and that you're left with the foundations of a great talk.

I think about planning separated into a few distinct parts, and I'm going to take you through all of them.

1. First up, think about your message. Why are you speaking, what is your purpose? What is the most important thing you want people to take away from their time with you?
2. Next is the audience. Who are they? Why are they listening to you? What are their motivations, hopes, fears and goals?
3. Then we're going to think about why this audience should care about what you have to say. How can you make it relevant or interesting to them?
4. Next we're going to explore your key ingredients. What is the essential information your audience needs to hear to follow your thinking and to arrive at the conclusion you want them to?
5. Finally we're going to think about *you*. We want to craft a talk that only you could give, so we're going to dig deep regarding who you are, and your unique perspective that makes this message and these stories worth hearing from you, rather than from anybody else.

If you start by taking the time to consider these five things, it's hard to get it too wrong. But, conversely, without thinking about them enough or at all, it's easy to walk away from your opportunity to speak with a sense that you didn't quite use it to its full potential. You want to speak so others listen – that's why you're reading this book, so by taking the 'thinking part' seriously before you sit down and write a single word, you're going to vastly increase the chances that your message will resonate with the people you're speaking to.

You never know, you might surprise yourself and find that, once you've done this part of the work, your focus is actually on something completely different to what you initially thought it was. This is just as exciting and creative a stage of the process as putting your speech together, designing your slides or choosing your outfit, trust me!

All of the five stages are equally vital to producing great work, and it's important to do them in order as you get familiar with this process. It is iterative, so this may mean going back to an earlier stage once you've figured out things that need to change, but at least get your brain thinking about them in this order to begin with.

One
What is your big idea?

Whether you're presenting in a meeting, pitching for new business, asking your boss for a promotion or you're doing a TEDx talk, the one thing you have to be clear on is the same. What's your big idea? Knowing this will enable you to bring much-needed focus and clarity to what you're saying, which is why it's the first step in the planning process.

You might have no sense at all of where to begin, but, equally, the problem might be that you have *too many* ideas, or rather too many things you want the audience to take away. Both of these situations mean you'll need to be making editorial decisions about how to prioritise and structure your content. If you find yourself absolutely drowning in things you want to share, the process will be about trying to separate the ideas from the supporting evidence. What is the core message that runs through all the data and anecdotes and stories that binds them all together? That's the big idea: the data and anecdotes and stories aren't, themselves, the big idea.

So, first things first: ask yourself what is the *one* idea that you want your audience to leave with. Knowing this will help you both focus and determine everything from your storytelling to your structure to your planning, and, more than that, it will help you achieve the things you're trying to do with your talk, conversation or story.

I know it's not an easy task. Both in my capacity as a TEDx curator and in my work more generally as a speaking coach, I spend *hours* talking with people, going around in conversational circles and meanders and loops, trying to find *that idea* that sticks. When I say that, it may sound as if this is a failure on the part of a speaker or their idea or their content, but the opposite is actually true. That journey, being willing to do the exploratory phase of generating the right idea, is an integral part of creating an ultimately successful talk. It's like peeling an onion: sometimes you simply have to go through all the individual little layers to get right to the centre of the thing. The one great idea didn't just present itself to you – it needed to be revealed layer by layer, and challenging yourself to do the work to get to that point is really worth doing.

Finding your idea by looking at your theme through *your* lens is an intrinsic part of the process. We'll talk about this more a little further down the line (if you want to read more about that now, have a look at the section 'Finding your authentic voice', see p. 158), but it can be helpful to think about it a little at the 'big idea' stage too. Ask yourself what you're bringing to the table. I mean that in terms of your perspective, your expertise, your background, your unique personality. If I've asked you to speak at an event, I could have asked *anyone* to speak on your area of expertise, but I've chosen you. Why? What is it that you're bringing to this idea that someone else might not be able to? Whether it's science, business leadership, climate change, music, marketing, human rights – what do you personally bring to this idea? How does your perspective help you locate that great idea and create a talk that no one but you could deliver? What you want to avoid is creating a talk that you could hand to someone else to deliver and have it still work. It should feel like it's unique to you, and a lot of that will come from the perspective that you bring.

Find your focus

When you're presented with a longer-form speaking opportunity, there's an understandable temptation to want to include absolutely everything. So often we operate with a scarcity mindset, where we fear we'll never have the same opportunity again. But, instead, I would encourage you to operate with an abundance mindset and believe that this is just one of many opportunities you'll have to share your thoughts and ideas. This will hopefully make it easier for you to do some judicious editing, and allow you to cut things that might be great material but don't fit precisely with your one big idea and the trajectory of the argument you're trying to make.

Think of it as being on a mission to speak. All the decisions you're going to make when putting together this speech should be in service of that mission, and as few *other* missions as humanly possible. Neil Vora, masterful science communicator, TED speaker and specialist in pandemic prevention, who served for nearly a decade with the US Centers for Disease Control and Prevention (CDC), calls it your 'SOCO', or 'single overriding communication objective'. 'On day one of our media training at the CDC, they said, *Whenever you do any engagement with the media, know what your SOCO is.* So, that way, even if the interview or the talk goes in various different directions, I can always come back to my SOCO.'

Neil and the CDC are by no means the only people to think of it like this. Chris Anderson, the Head of TED, talks about a *'throughline, the connecting theme that ties together each narrative element'* in his book *TED Talks*. LGBT+ activist, climate communicator and drag queen Pattie Gonia echoes this, but has added another layer: feelings. 'I think the process that gets there is to have a North Star of a final emotion that I want people to feel. From that emotion I also think about the one-line message that I want people to take away from this. So there's an emotional response I want, and there's a message, and I build everything from there.'

If you're familiar with the world of marketing, it's similar to the 'think, feel, do' framework when looking at how an audience responds to a message. What do you want your audience to think, feel and do after they listen to you?

Give your idea the space to shine

Esha Bhandari, a human rights lawyer who has argued in front of the US Supreme Court, mentioned to me how vital it is to overcome the desire to 'show your work'. 'The preparation you do ahead of oral arguments might cover a lot of points and issues that you never actually speak about, because you keep it to your themes,' she told me. 'But the only reason you could get to your themes is because you did the preparatory work in advance and you know these are your most persuasive points. One mistake I see sometimes is that people have done a tonne of preparation work, you've read a thousand articles or a thousand cases, and then when you get up to speak, you feel like you have to show your work. That's not actually the most effective in most cases. You don't have to show your work. What you have to do is distil the two or three key points from everything you read and hammer them home on those, knowing that you've read the gazillion articles, so you have the information to back it up.'

When I'm working with TED and TEDx speakers specifically, this is a situation where you could literally be talking about *anything*. They've been approached because they broadly have expertise in a certain area, or maybe they just seem like an interesting person. Maybe they've come to our conversation with a kernel of an idea, but generally it's a big blank slate. Infinite possibilities. If you've found yourself in this position, where you've been asked to speak but aren't quite sure what you should speak about, the way I encourage them – and you – to think about it is like a Venn diagram. One circle is your knowledge: the things you have spent your life becoming an expert in. And then the other circle is all the things you care about, the things you're passionate about, the things that keep you up at night. When you figure out what's sitting in the overlap between those two things, that's when you've found your big idea.

Maybe you have a trusted friend you can talk your ideas out with, or, failing that, maybe sit down with a notebook and scribble down everything you want to share, every interesting anecdote that proves the thing you're trying to explain to your audience, the research that you wish more people understood. Make notes, diagrams, drawings, whatever it takes to help you dig and excavate until you find that diamond, the central proposition around which everything else will coalesce. You want to think of the process like a funnel, where you're trying to reduce and refine down to the core element that constitutes your big idea. You might start with a vast topic like online safety or immigration policy, but the purpose of this process is to funnel it all down so it gets narrower and more specific.

Avoid trying to 'inspire'

There's one mission or objective I would definitely try to avoid, however. Something I encounter a lot in my work is the idea that talks, speeches and stories should be 'inspiring'. It's an idea that comes through a lot on social media, with vulnerable and emotional moments perfectly calibrated to achieve virality. It's tempting to make 'inspiring' the goal, but when you're formulating your big idea, I would caution against *trying* to make it inspiring. Whenever I'm working with clients and they tell me they want to deliver an 'inspiring' speech, I have to sit them down and give them the bad news that this isn't how it works. You do not *give* an inspiring story. People might *get* inspired by a story. It's an audience-centred thing and you can't necessarily control it. You need your own purpose, your own mission, your own story, and the audience will respond to it on their terms. Your job is to find the thing you care so much about – that one big idea – and communicate it in a way that makes it feel so infectious, so curiosity-provoking, so compelling that it makes your audience want to change their beliefs or practices. When you're trying to develop your idea, it's easy to watch a bunch of TED talks at home and see an inspiring speaker and think 'I want to be like *that*, I want to inspire people like *that*', but inspiration is not an emotion. Worse still, it can have the exact opposite effect, giving your audience the impression you're just in it to be 'inspiring' and actually don't have a compelling idea to share. Think of every caricature of a motivational speaker you've ever seen: you don't want to be that guy!

In the words of neuroscientist Kris De Meyer in his brilliant TED talk, 'Feeling stuck on climate change? Here's what to do': 'Emotions are simply not predictable drivers of action. Thinking that you can pull some emotional strings and some action will pop out, that's really not how people work.'

We all have the desire to be heard, to be listened to. After all, that's why this book is called *How to Speak So Others Listen*! But it's not just *ourselves* that we want people to listen to, it's the ideas that we want to share, the ideas that we believe might move the needle for someone out there who hears us. Some of the most interesting ideas might not be the most obvious ones. I recommend getting messy: remember what I said about me and my TEDx speakers having long, meandering conversations in and around their area of expertise to find their idea?

Corey Hajim, a writer, editor – but most relevantly here – former Business Curator for TED, likes to think of this phase as like a closet clearout. 'I love cleaning out closets, and I feel like when I work with someone, we look at *everything* in the closet. It's like a big brain dump, and then I help them organise it and get rid of things so that they can see what they have and what's most special in that closet.'

A question is not an idea

Although it might feel tempting to frame your big idea as a question, this is not the right approach. If you do have a question that you think is at the core of your idea, then your big idea is going to be the *answer* to that question, rather than the question itself.

When we're thinking about TED talks in particular, it's useful to remember that the 'title' of the talk you see online on the TED website or YouTube is not the same as the 'big idea' in the talk. It's easy to get these things confused, but think of the title as more of a marketing tool, whereas the big idea is the actual substance of what you want people to take away from the talk. You don't create the title first and then create the talk: you create the talk first, and the title second. Think of the title as marketing first and foremost rather than the substance of what you're trying to share.

Keep your eyes focused on your mission, and let that guide you to the central idea that will best enable you to share that mission with your audience. Whether it's influencing their beliefs, attitude or behaviours, you will be able to look within your knowledge and experience to find the perfect idea. The truth is, your audience will only meaningfully take away one or maybe two things from what you say to them, so you need to do the work to decide what you want those to be.

But what's an idea without an audience?

Two
Who are you talking to?

Now you've figured out your key message, you might think the work is done and you can start writing. In fact, lots of people stop planning here. But you're not going to stop, because now you've got to start thinking about your audience.

Neglect your audience at your peril. If you craft a talk that's inappropriate for your specific audience, the best-case scenario is that people find you boring and annoying and irrelevant. And the worst-case scenario? Your audience finds you outright disrespectful. This is true whether you're speaking to one person or to a whole auditorium, and we all know what it feels like to be in dialogue with someone who's only thinking about themselves. It doesn't feel great.

Thinking about your audience is absolutely transformative for public speakers. Briar Goldberg, the Director of Coaching for TED, has found making this the foundation of someone's talk has a huge impact on their effectiveness. 'You can coach people all day long, but where I've seen the biggest transformations and where my coaching sessions certainly get more effective is when the speaker starts sitting in the audience's shoes. All of a sudden when people start to truly understand

and put themselves in the position of the person receiving their message, you start to see the world of effective communication differently.'

This is not to say that once you know who your audience is, you're just meant to cater every second of content to what they believe or what they want to hear. After all, you spent valuable time crafting *your* big idea, honing that 'SOCO' (single overriding core objective), as Neil Vora put it in the previous section. First you figure out what you want to say, and then you do the work to understand the audience that's actually going to be in front of you. Stage three of the process is about aligning your core message with your audience, but you can't get to that stage without thinking about the audience in the first place.

But what does it mean to think about your audience? Consider this the next time you find yourself in a one-to-one conversation with someone you haven't met before. We think about our audience intuitively in situations like this by picking up on their cues and jumping on them, talking more about something that we know is interesting to them, or moving away from a subject we can tell is making them uncomfortable or boring them.

Listening to your audience can be such a powerful way to find gaps in the information or content they're seeing elsewhere, and figuring out whether you're the person to fill those gaps. Helen Tupper and Sarah Ellis are career experts, and together they host a podcast called *Squiggly Careers* and are the founders of Amazing If, a company with a mission to make careers better for everyone. When I had the chance to speak with them, Sarah told me how their ability to get feedback from their audience is one of the key ingredients of their success. 'I think Helen and I are good at noticing what sticks,' she told me. 'We are talking to so many people every single week, all of the time, so you start to notice what sticks. For example, lots of our clients at the moment are saying to us that performance really matters, we want a high-performing company, we want a high-performing team. And we notice that and then we go, *Hmm, should we spend a bit of time on what that might mean for us?* Or we notice that, in all of our online workshops, people love it when we say, *Create, don't wait for your career,* because everyone gives us heart emojis and they rewrite it in the chat. And you think, *Okay, there's something in that.* I think we are good at sensing and noticing what's sticking, what's standing out; what do people repeat back to us. When we first shared the idea of squiggly, we weren't saying, *Squiggly is the thing.* We just drew a diagram that was an image of a staircase and an image of a squiggle as an introduction to strengths and values and all this other stuff that we wanted to talk about. And everyone was like, *Whoa, whoa, whoa, what's that?* You're getting loads of nods. You're getting loads of immediate feedback.' Thinking of everything you do as being like a conversation, where you're intuitively open to those cues, will help you build content that resonates more with your audience.

My friend, Director of Facilitation at Beyond Equality and my co-host on the *Climate Curious* podcast, Ben Hurst, who does a *lot* of public speaking, largely around masculinity and often to boys in schools (so a tough subject with a difficult crowd), agrees that thinking about your audience is the key to getting your message to resonate: 'I think where I see a lot of people in my work going wrong is that you can have all of the content correct and perfect, but it just doesn't connect,' he said. 'And the connection is transformative for people. So, I think it's all about that first skill of being able to read a room. Sometimes I walk into a room and I can see that nobody wants to be there, and everybody hates it. And so, I'll ask some questions, like, *Who's here by choice? Has anybody been forced to be here?* I'm trying to find the points of relevance so that people can kind of relax into the knowledge that they're safe.' Ben is generally full of wisdom, and he also reminded me that it's important not to take on too many assumptions about the audience before we've even encountered them, especially if we're really deeply attached to our core message and want it to resonate. 'I have to challenge my own assumptions about who wants to hear what.'

Thinking about your audience means considering them when choosing the kind of language you use, whether that's more formal or less formal, more specialised language or less specialised language. It's about what you choose to wear on the day, it's about the cultural references you use in any stories or anecdotes. Vidhya Ramalingam, an expert in counter-terrorism extremism and the person behind the TED talk 'The real-world danger of online myths', is often engaged in public speaking and it's not always to an audience as large or as generalist as the TED audience. This means she has to make slight pivots every time to keep what she has to say feeling relevant and engaging. 'Even how I establish credibility looks different with each of those different audiences, whether it's tech companies, venture capitalists, foundations. So the story I tell about myself, the story I tell about the company, might be slightly different with each audience.'

Why are they listening?

One of the biggest factors when really thinking about your audience is not just the 'who' but the 'why'. Why is your audience there? Are they listening to you voluntarily or have they been told they have to listen to you? What level of knowledge do they have of your subject matter, and what do you know about theirs? If I'm coaching a physicist or a doctor, for example, and they're speaking to a room full of fellow physicists or doctors, they can assume a basic level of shared knowledge in the room which wouldn't be the case if they were speaking to a general audience. But you can go deeper than that: what unifies them? Do they share demographic or psychographic characteristics? For example, they could all be from the same part of the world or at the same point in their careers, or is there perhaps an ideology that unifies them?

This work is much easier to do with smaller groups and in informal settings, so I understand if it feels like an overwhelming task when you're about to take the stage at a big event! With smaller groups it's easier to be intuitive and modify your tone or approach based on what feedback the audience is giving you.

If the format allows, and it feels like more of a conversation than you having to stand there and speak with no feedback – say a more one-to-one situation – my advice is *always* to let the other person speak first. Always ask the first question, never give the first answer. Any question I can ask that allows the other person to tell me about themselves gives me a tonne of information that I can work with in the moment. This works really well at networking events or even meetings where everyone introduces themselves at the start – the more you know about who you're speaking to, the better you can tailor your information to them.

Again, this is not to say that I 'change' myself to please my audience. The core of my message and the substance of what I believe in does not change. I'm not trying to manipulate people or misrepresent myself, and it's actually not so much about modifying the 'what' but about modifying the 'how'.

What do I mean by that? Jodie Jackson, a great speaker I've worked with whose work revolves around mental clarity, productivity and well-being, meets with people ahead of time or produces a questionnaire to find out what's important to the group she's speaking to. She told me she does this to 'find little connection points'. If there's an anecdote or a news story that she realises will help her to connect with that specific group, for example, she'll make a small modification to her content. 'Sometimes that's the only tweak that I'll make to my entire talk. But it then makes them feel like, *Oh yeah!*'

If that doesn't sound like the right approach for your needs, you can also stealthily do this research by asking colleagues for as much information as possible. I work with a lot of people where the 'event' I'm preparing them for is presenting to a board of directors or trustees. The odds are, at least one other person in your organisation will have presented to them in the past, and that person will therefore be a goldmine of information on who this audience is. Why is the board there? Are they chosen for their expertise in this subject matter or because of their expertise in something else? Secondly, what are they meeting for? Is it to approve budgets for the thing you're working on or is it just to be informed of what's going on in your organisation and sector? And, thirdly, what is their temperament as a group of people? Some boards will ask you to present and they will sit quietly and listen to you and then there'll be dedicated time for questions afterwards. Others love to interrupt! That's their temperament as a group. So, think back to what I said about the *how* not the *what*: knowing that this audience interrupts will affect *how* you structure your content, not *what* the fundamentals of your content are. It will mean it's even more important to get your big messages out really, really fast and really, really clearly. Imagine you're going on TV and you only have 30 seconds to make your point before they cut to commercial (or, in this case, someone pipes up with a question).

Your audience are not psychopaths

We've all seen Simon Cowell tearing into some poor performer on stage or watched the dragons rip an idea apart on Dragon's Den. It's easy to think every audience is like this – but that is very rarely the case. One notable exception is the University of Chicago's economics department, who infamously used to hold seminars where the culture was to challenge everything the speaker said and try to find any hole in their argument. It's tough and it was regarded as one of the biggest trials by fire any economist can experience. But knowing this in advance allows presenters to prepare in a very different way than for a more supportive, gentle audience. And, this, more combative situation, is so rare that it has become a thing of legend, rather than it being a norm. Audiences are 99 per cent of the time on your side – they want you to succeed because they want to have a good experience too.

Clover Hogan, the climate activist and founder of the youth non-profit organisation Force of Nature, has some really interesting and thought-provoking things to say about the idea of adapting to your audience. 'In certain rooms, particularly if it's a closed-door room with a group of business leaders, I'm a lot more strategic in the way that I communicate, because they're that much further away from where I stand,' Clover told me. 'I think, with time, I learned it's not so much about trying to squeeze my message into jargon they'll understand, but just treating whoever you're speaking to as a human being, and acknowledging where they're coming from.'

In my experience the most difficult audience to tailor things to is the 'general public'. We'll talk more later in the book about curiosity, because there *are* things that stimulate almost every person's interest and keep them listening, but when approaching a more general audience, you are free to make a decision. Make a decision about who in the audience you most want to hear your message. Which group in particular are you trying to connect with? When you tailor it like that, other people hear it too, but when you don't tailor it to anyone at all, it can feel kind of meaningless, or at least unfocused. To go back to the meal analogy I used on page 12 it's like trying to cook a meal for absolutely everyone. You can't do it! How are you going to please everyone if some people are halal, vegan, gluten-free, low-sodium? A celery stick? That doesn't sound very fun. Say you make a spicy vegan dish. Non-vegans can eat it too, and the people who don't like spice can add some yoghurt, it's not the end of the world. But *you* have to make a decision, and that decision should always be in service of your audience and your message.

In the end, we want to be approaching every choice in this process strategically. Choosing the right message was the first step, and now tailoring that message so it'll be heard by the right people is the second.

Now that you've taken the time to think about your audience, let's move on.

Three

Why should they care?

You care. Of course you care. It's your area of expertise, the idea you're passionate about, the project you're pitching for, the thing you're asking for money to fund. But the fact you care isn't always enough when it comes to public speaking and storytelling. When I say 'care', I know that means a lot of different things to different people, and maybe that isn't the word you would personally use. If 'care' doesn't resonate with you specifically, then think instead about how you make your content relevant to the audience that's in front of you.

You're not speaking into a vacuum, or looking in a mirror: you've got an audience, and you've got to make *them* care too. Now, you might want to jump straight to this – the third stage of a five-point planning process – and start thinking about how to convince your listeners to care as much as you do, but may I reiterate that this is the *third stage*. It's impossible to do this part of the process well while skipping the first two steps! You need to first know what your idea is (the thing you're asking them to care about, your 'big idea', your SOCO) and who 'they' are (see the previous section, on audience).

In short, when we ask 'why should they care?', you need to be clear on who *they* are and what you're asking *them* to care about. Until you work through those previous two steps, you cannot even begin to understand how you make your big idea feel relevant to them.

The more you understand about your audience, the more you can figure out how to tailor your message to increase the chances of making them care. So, if your audience is already quite knowledgeable about your message, you can speak more specifically in pursuit of that goal. Conversely, an audience that is starting from very little knowledge and might feel quite far away from your 'big idea' may struggle more to connect with the ideas you're dealing with. Trying to create a sense of urgency might work with a group of people who are already clear on the issues at play, but will leave someone who's new to the subject feeling baffled, and won't necessarily help you achieve your purpose. If I'm trying to make something feel urgent to you, it has to already be in your orbit somehow: I can't just present you with totally new information and ask you to care about it *right here, right now*.

Actions inspire more actions

An idea I learned from the neuroscientist Kris De Meyer is that we mistakenly think that belief, care or concern become action, when, in fact, it is the other way around. That, instead, when we start taking action, beliefs become more profound and ingrained. Telling stories about people taking action, making it seem as if action is possible to your audience, making them understand the actions they are able to take, will have a huge impact on them, more so than just trying to get them to care. I actually think this is so vital that I'm co-hosting a podcast with filmmaker Matt Golding about people taking action to make positive change in their local areas. We're talking to a community in Bristol who built their own wind turbine and a community in Shropshire who brought together 8,000 people from around the world to buy back their farm from developers – stories not just of *what* people did, but *how* they did it, so others can have an idea of what's possible and how to achieve it. As Kris De Meyer puts it, 'it's about giving people the recipes, not just showing them the menu.'

Your audience is giving you the most precious thing they have, which is their time and attention, and it's up to you to capitalise on that. Clover Hogan, a climate activist I've supported with her TED and TEDx talks, put it this way: 'The biggest evolution for me has been realising that to be an effective communicator, you first need to understand what people care about, what they're motivated by, what the problems are or challenges are that they face day to day, and then how, as a communicator, can you be that bridge between where that person is and the idea or perspective, whatever you want to plant.'

The idea of bridging a gap brings me on to the idea of curiosity. Maybe even more importantly, stories poke at our natural inclination towards curiosity. Curiosity may have killed the cat, but it certainly motivates many of our decisions in everyday life! Just think of clickbait headlines – do you really care 'which child star of the '90s looks UNRECOGNISABLE now'? Do you really think your fortune is going to be found by clicking on '21 money-making secrets the banks DON'T want you to know'? Probably not! But that's not what's motivating you to click. What's motivating you is curiosity. Something is happening in an irrational, profoundly human part of your brain, even when your rational brain knows it doesn't care. George Loewenstein is one of the most influential researchers into curiosity, and suggests in his paper, 'The Psychology of Curiosity', that curiosity is a kind of 'deprivation that arises from the perception of a gap in knowledge and understanding'. He suggests that this information gap – between what we know and what we want to know – works in the same way as other drive states, such as hunger. The desire to close the information gap is still strong, he finds, even when the unknown information is of absolutely no importance, just like those clickbait headlines. He proposes that there are four main situations that really trigger our curiosity: questions or puzzles; sequences of events with an anticipated but unknown resolution; a defiance of our expectations; and knowing someone else possesses knowledge that we do not yet know. We want to be putting your audience in a position where you spark off that desire to know more, *and* give them the tools to learn along with you.

As well as triggering their curiosity, the best way to get your audience to care is, fundamentally, by crafting compelling content, by being a master of your field of expertise, by choosing the right stories, the right examples, the right data and then presenting it all in the right structure to really bring it all to life for them. It's the same logic as the difference between 'fake it til you make it' and real confidence: by writing a great talk or presentation or pitch that hits all those factors just right, you're more likely to enthuse your audience than by just hoping that your personal passion is enough to convince them. Imagine you're trying to get your boss to give you a promotion. Sure, you're passionate about it, but ask yourself what you need to do to make them passionate about the idea too. In practice, this means tailoring your content to the needs of your audience: understand and anticipate the things that this specific group of people might be interested in or concerned about, and try to angle your content to capture those concerns and interests. For example, if you're a climate communicator but, on this occasion, you're speaking to an animal welfare organisation, how can you angle your climate content to encapsulate the environmental impact on animals?

In the previous section, I mentioned that speakers often make the mistake of trying to go too general in order to appeal to a broader audience. This comes up again when thinking about why your audience should care, and how to get them to care. David Biello, science journalist and Climate Curator at TED, explains it like this: 'Specifics are actually the key to universality. So it's not so much that you and I have both been to the specific woods that I like to walk through in the Adirondacks that I'm going to include in my talk on nature-based solutions to climate change, but you've walked through some woods. Weirdly, having those specific details that *this was my experience as I was walking through the Adirondacks and I encountered this pine tree* ... that seems like you're closing off universality, when actually you're opening it up. You're giving people hooks where they're like, *Oh, yes, I too have had an experience with a tree.*'

One of the best talks I can think of to illustrate the question 'Why should they care?' is Dan Gilbert's 2014 TED talk, which is called 'The psychology of your future self'. This is almost certainly not going to be the last time I reference it in this book, because it's just so great! Dan takes the subject where he is an expert – the psychology of decision-making and judgement – and immediately makes it feel both relevant and accessible to his audience. He could have pitched it completely differently, started by talking about his experience, why he's an authority on the subject, reeled off some facts and figures from his own extensive research career. Maybe that would have appealed to the small percentage of people in the

> audience who were decision-making geeks or already had some knowledge of his work, and the rest would have walked away thinking that it wasn't really for them. But, instead, he intentionally sparks the audience's curiosity in a way that makes it near impossible for them to disengage with one simple question: 'why do we make decisions that our future selves so often regret?' He pitched it just right, and turned what could feel like an inaccessible topic into something irresistible, because he considered his audience and what they care about – in this case themselves and their future.

Your passion and enthusiasm makes it *feel* obvious that your audience should care, but you can't rely on that alone. So how are you going to meet your audience where they're at, and try to bring them to where you're at? If you really can't figure out a solution, may I suggest watching Dan Gilbert's TED talk *again*, and realising that the way he hooks the audience in at the beginning is by getting them to think about themselves through that first fundamental question. People love thinking about themselves! If you can't get the audience to care any other way, then figure out a way to make it all about them. That's a little speaking hack for you.

Let's think about this book. When I sat down to write it, I didn't decide I just wanted to list off all the clever things I have to say about public speaking and storytelling and that you, the reader, would just have to listen to them because I care about them. Instead, I thought strategically about who *you* might be, what your concerns might be, where you might be coming from, and tried to apply my own knowledge and passion to the needs of the reader – you. That's how I'm trying to get you to think about this part of the planning process: that magic combination of what you want to share, and the people you want to share it with.

We're making good progress through my five-point planning checklist! Now we're ready to start thinking about your key ingredients . . .

Four

What are your key ingredients?

Okay, we're getting closer! You've done the big-picture work – the really broad strokes elements, like what your point is, who you're speaking to – then you've got a bit more in-depth and thought about how you're going to bring those two things together. Now it's time to think about the finer details. Think back to the analogy I used when talking about the three steps to giving a great talk: you know you have to cook a meal, you know who you're feeding the meal to, you know what recipe you're going to make. That means you've been able to write an ingredients list. Say you're making spaghetti and meatballs: you've written down 'tomatoes'. Now, think of this part of the planning process as like being in the supermarket, deciding *what kind* of tomatoes you're buying. That's right, we're getting specific.

All I want you to do is figure out what the key ingredients are to your talk, presentation, pitch, conversation, whatever you're preparing for right now. What are the facts that are absolutely essential to communicating your message? I'm talking about the case studies, the statistics, the analogies that really throw light on your subject and will lodge themselves firmly in the memories of your audience. The one thing we're *still* not doing is thinking about how to combine those ingredients, so don't worry about that just yet.

Before you dive into the assembly phase, putting all of these ideas together, make sure you're clear on the essential information your audience needs, and how this information helps them to follow your narrative. It might be helpful to think of this in terms of the evidence you want to supply to get the audience to be 'on your side', so to speak.

Simon Bucknall, a public speaking expert whose opinions I'm so interested in that I do a podcast *on public speaking* with him, suggests taking a step back at this point if you feel clear on your overarching message, but don't necessarily feel you have the stories to back it up. He recommends asking yourself: 'How do I know that's true? What have I seen, felt, believed or experienced that backs that up?' In essence, what are the stories that led *you* to the place you're in now, whether they're experiences you've personally had, or facts or stories you were told that led you to that conclusion.

Keep it simple

It's important you don't lose sight of the 'key' in 'key ingredients', though. When you've got a message you're passionate about and an audience willing to listen, I know it's tempting to throw in everything, including the kitchen sink. Something I often find myself saying to my speaking clients is this: imagine you're standing on one side of a stream and the audience is on the other side of the stream. Your job is to lay down paving stones to get them from where they are to where you are. If you lay down too few, or lay them out in a weird configuration, they're not going to cross the stream. They're going to be like 'noooo, I'm gonna fall in the stream', and who can blame them? But if you lay down too many, they can end up wandering off in any direction: they don't actually have to come to meet *you* where you are. So you need to pick the paving stones that are enough in quantity, appropriate for the ability of the audience, and *just enough* of them to get them to you without letting them get distracted or bored. Think of this part of the process as pitching everything at the right level for your audience (again, the secret sauce is thinking about your audience!), giving enough but not too much information, and always, always tailoring it for this specific group of people.

Because what constitutes a 'key ingredient' will almost certainly be different depending on who you're speaking to. An audience with a similar level of knowledge to you will require fewer metaphorical paving stones than one that hasn't encountered your area of expertise before.

What is the most economical you can be with the statistics you have in service of your message? What anecdotes will most elegantly illuminate your point without leaving your audience scratching their heads as to their relevance? What's the least amount of extra *stuff* you can include while still getting your point across?

This idea of editing yourself is an issue that often arises with speakers I work with who have a really extensive body of work, or have worked in a sector for a really long time. It can feel overwhelming to look at your area of expertise, the thing you're the most passionate and knowledgeable about, and think 'I just have too much here, I don't even know how to cut this down'. Think of this as the time that you become an editor of your own knowledge, and try to match the stories, facts and figures to the specific points you want to make in service of your one big idea.

Kumi Naidoo, the former director of Greenpeace and current President of the Fossil Fuel Non-Proliferation Treaty Initiative, explained it to me like this: 'I'm not saying be simplistic. I'm saying be accessible.' This really illuminated something for me. It's not just about saying things simply, it's about figuring out what to say and how to say it in a way that will resonate with your audience because they understand it.

And if you can't break your big idea down into its constituent parts yet, now is the time to do it. Workshop ways of explaining it that are so clear and logical that even someone who's never encountered it before will understand. That will help you narrow down the essential ingredients to communicate that message. It might be worth thinking about the things that changed *your* mind or convinced *you* about this subject. It might even be worth including an anecdote about how, once upon a time, you thought differently about it, but this fact or this figure radically repositioned it for you! But that's up to you – I'm not telling you what your key ingredients are, as only you can know that.

> To help you think about the kind of thing I'm talking about, here are a few elements you could use in a talk about climate change:
>
> Statistics – A survey conducted by the UN Development Programme with the University of Oxford and GeoPoll, for example, showed that 80 per cent of people globally want their governments to take stronger action to tackle the climate crisis. This fact could help illustrate a point about how action on climate change is more politically popular than we have been led to believe.
>
> Story – Here is an example of a story Kumi Naidoo (whom I just mentioned above) told me that could help illuminate the need to make climate change feel relevant and accessible to more people: 'When I was at Greenpeace in 2011, I occupied an oil rig in the Arctic. The slogan that we were carrying said *Stop Arctic Destruction*. And at that point in 2011, fewer people in the world than today understood that the Arctic serves as a refrigerator and the air conditioner of the planet. And in the summer months now in the Arctic, we are having lower and lower levels of Arctic sea ice. At the time, 99.99 per cent of the people in the world didn't know what that meant, but we felt good about it. So I

> got arrested, I was in prison for about a week, and then I got back home to South Africa a couple of weeks later. And one of the kids in the family says to me, *What a stupid slogan, you activists are constantly speaking to yourselves. You don't think about where people are. What does the average person on the African continent know about the Arctic? It's so far from them. It's like a different cultural and geographical reality.* Then I said, *What would have been a better slogan?* And she said, *Well, I'm not paid to come up with slogans, but, for starters, 'Save Santa Claus Now' would be a much better slogan.'*
>
> Analogy – When I talked to Nathalie McDermott, founder and co-CEO of Heard, a narrative change organisation working to shift how social issues are portrayed in popular culture, she used a really great analogy of an orchestra in the context of climate change. 'If you look at media output as an orchestra, until now you've just had the brass section banging away about climate, going, *it's awful.* So awareness is raised but it's loud, so audiences are doing one of two things: we're moving to the other rooms because it's too loud, or we're just getting used to the noise, and we're just zoning out.'

So that's step four done. Just one more left, and then it's time to put it all together . . .

Five

What is your unique perspective?

Phew! You've made it to step five of five, and I really hope this is the easiest one of them all, because it's all about *you*. This last stage is where we think about why you're the best person to deliver your message.

We can break this idea down into two main questions. Firstly, what unique perspective do you have on this topic? And, secondly, what is it about this idea that makes you so fired up?

On the first point, I want you to think about all your unique experiences, all the things that have happened to you, your knowledge, your qualifications, your ideas, and smush them all together. Then, by some magic, that smushed substance gets transformed into a lens. When you look through that lens at your big idea, how does it change what you see? What can only you see? What sticks out?

Take marketing, for example. There are probably thousands of people in London right now who could give a passable talk on the topic. What is it about *you* that makes your perspective on marketing so unique that only you could deliver it? Because that's what all this is about: what we're trying to avoid is a situation where you've written a clear and coherent speech, but it's so generic that it could be delivered by absolutely anyone. Instead we're trying to create a situation where it's so specific to you that it only works *because* it's being delivered by you.

Now, I'm going to give you two pieces of advice that may seem contradictory. Don't remove yourself from the story, but don't feel like you have to make it *about* you. You don't have to reveal personal or private information in service of bringing your unique perspective to your talk. I think a lot of people shy away from storytelling because they think that necessarily means telling personal stories. But, instead, what I try to get people to do is think about the stories they can tell that are beyond themselves.

Passion is contagious

What I mean when I say not to remove yourself from the story is that your emotions are often contagious. Think back to the third point in our five-point checklist, where we were trying to get your audience to care. Enthusiasm is infectious, so if you're excited, you should let that come through. If you're feeling angry or scared out of your mind about climate change, it's okay to let that influence you. One of my public speaking clients was an expert in the electrification of the US energy grid. My job was to help him put together a really tight eight-minute speech that was compelling and would help him raise funds to do this work, and I'm going to level with you: I just thought *oh no*. How was I going to do this? How could I turn something as vast, as dense, as high-level, and as frankly dry as the electrification of the US energy grid into content that was so compelling that people would want to throw money at it? I just didn't think I could do it. Well, it turns out this guy was so passionately in love with his topic that, after speaking to him for a matter of minutes, I discovered I was, in fact, passionately in love with the topic too. I am now a zealous advocate for US grid electrification! I can talk about it endlessly, with confidence, and am able to share information that I never in a million years believed I would remember. And it's all because this person let his geeky passion shine through. So don't for one minute think you have to hold back and keep everything in the realm of the formal. I've watched people I've found *fascinating* in one-on-one conversations transform into utterly bland and forgettable speakers before my very eyes, and when I ask them what happened, it's almost always because they thought they needed to be more formal, more academic, more serious for people to listen to them, when I know that they're brimming with enthusiasm that would have – should have – been completely irresistible to the audience.

Being yourself without revealing everything

I completely understand the impulse to rein it in. People with marginalised identities may have a harder time both seeing themselves and being seen by others as an authority, so the idea of letting your real self shine through may feel difficult or unnatural, depending on who you are. Sophie Williams, an author and anti-racist advocate I've worked with as a TED speaker, told me: 'The way that certain groups are perceived, when they speak out for themselves or they advocate for themselves, is very different if they're from different marginalised identities. Women, and especially Black women, face this sort of dislikeability, and not being believed when we tell our own stories.' We'll talk about the idea of your own authentic voice later in the book, but I just wanted to say that I totally get it if the thought of *being yourself* in a public way feels vulnerable or exposing.

Your audience wants to feel like they know you, but you don't have to achieve that by revealing personal information. Maybe, for you, that looks like lifting the curtain, exposing a little something of the closed rooms that the audience might not ever get to see inside but which you have access to. What are the things that you know, what perspective can you bring, that might allow your audience to feel like you're offering them a glimpse of something unique?

Maryam Pasha

You've got your idea. You know your audience. You know why they should care about what you care about. You know the key ingredients you want to deploy in service of your big idea. You know what makes you the perfect messenger for this big idea. I think you're ready to start putting it all together . . .

Section 2
Assembly

Why storytelling is so effective

Of course, first and foremost, this is a public speaking book, and you're probably reading it because you have an opportunity to speak that you want to prepare for. But before we get into the practical bits about how to put your speech or presentation together, I also want to help you to understand quite how powerful a tool storytelling can be in this setting. My goal is to convince you that you should use the structures of storytelling as well as stories themselves every time you speak.

Stories are, put simply, an elegant way of making information memorable. And isn't that, after all, your goal? To keep *your* information in the minds of the audience. To make it memorable. The social psychologist Jonathan Haidt notably referred to our brains as a 'story processor, not a logic processor' in his 2012 book *The Righteous Mind*. It benefits us to create stories around information in order to have that information better understood by our audience. The human brain loves patterns, and a story is a way to transform information into a pattern that we find easier to process and internalise.

Helen Tupper, who speaks to big audiences (including TEDx) on a regular basis as the co-founder of Amazing If – an award-winning company with a mission to make careers better for everyone – clarified this for me very neatly: 'I think the role that stories play is to create connection with our audience quickly. They're also a leveller, because I think when you are speaking in the type of speaking that we do, we're speaking from a position of authority on careers. So the risk is that you're seen as unrelatable because you've been given this stage, virtual or real, and I think that can create a little bit of disconnection. You tell a story so you can make a very quick connection with people.'

Storytelling enables us to take a concept in the abstract, which might be hard to understand or to communicate in its pure form, and helps to turn the same concept into something memorable, accessible and maybe even shareable. Once we understand the fact that stories are powerful, we can attempt to harness that power for good. A paper published in the *Environmental Research Letters* journal in January 2021 by Kris De Meyer, Emily Coren, Mark McCaffrey and Cheryl Slean is a great example of this. Titled 'Transforming the stories we tell about climate change: from "issue" to "action"', it lays out the approach of using storytelling to effect change. What it proposes is quite simple: taking an approach to climate communication based on a variety of stories of people taking *positive* action on climate change, which in turn leaves the listener feeling empowered to do the same, rather than feeling overwhelmed by fear. The facts remain the same, but this shift takes climate change from an 'issue-based' problem to an 'action-based' one. The paper sums up what you want from an opportunity to speak: for your audience to leave that experience with the urge to *do something* – preferably something good, in service of your message.

It's something that many activists and people engaged in social change already know well: that you can have all the relevant and accurate information in the world that shows *why* your issue is important, but it's often stories that move the needle, rather than cold, hard facts. Stories have the power to build empathy, help to shift mindsets and open up new possibilities, all of which are crucial to doing meaningful work with social purpose. The comedian Sofie Hagen put it to me in a simple way that I really loved: 'Storytelling is my way of making sense of the world. Most of the things I say on stage, the point of it all is me saying, *Hello, am I alone in this? Is it just me?*'

Using stories in two ways

I think about storytelling in two ways when it comes to public speaking: you can use storytelling structures (like *in medias res* or Nancy Duarte's Sparklines – we'll come to those later) to help you think about the flow and the order of the information you want to share. But you can also use these structures (like Hero's Journey or the Pixar Pitch – again, you'll learn more about these soon!) to *create* a story that you use in your public speaking, which has key elements, like a character with an objective who undergoes a transformation.

You can do both of these things at the same time, or just one. I like to think of it as story as structure, and story as story.

> Vidhya Ramalingam, the founder and CEO of Moonshot, a company using technology to end online harms, has found storytelling absolutely crucial to the success of this extremely important goal.
>
> > The reason why we landed on storytelling was that for years at Moonshot, even though we're a company, the people who come to work here aren't driven by making money. They work here because they care about the issues. So one of our biggest challenges has been business development, or sales. Sales is seen as an icky word, you think of door-to-door salesmen, and that's not what we are. So we've been trying to almost rebrand sales within Moonshot as something that feels much more relatable to everyone and where they understand why it is we're doing it. Sales is the lifeblood of the business, and it's how we are able to keep having an impact. One of the reasons why we latched on to storytelling was we realised that, ultimately, if you distil sales down to one core thing, it's storytelling. You have to be able to sell who you are, sell the work and sell us as an organisation, and to do that, you have to tell compelling stories.

At the most basic level, a story is a story because something changed. Something is different between the beginning of the story and the end of it – otherwise, it's not really a story, it's just a statement. If 'once upon a time' is the beginning, then the story is about how we get to the 'happy ever after'. Story lives in that change, that adventure, those peaks and troughs, that tension and range of emotions.

And it's worth saying that thinking about storytelling will almost certainly make your public speaking life easier, and that's what this book is all about, right? Jodie Jackson, an expert on unlocking human potential, has seen the difference that storytelling has made to her public speaking. 'I used to literally bring a script into the classroom with me because I thought the content mattered so much and I had to get it perfect,' she told me. 'I had to remember *this* or I had to say *that*, and then I realised stories are easier from a communication point of view because they're easier to remember. They don't rely on so much specific detail, you can ad lib a lot easier, and they're a great way to engage people and make it feel relevant.'

Stories are sticky

The need for your content to be memorable is particularly acute when you're one of several people speaking at a particular event. For example, if your public speaking engagement is a pitch to an investor who is seeing you plus ten other companies in one afternoon, or a job interview where you're up against several candidates, a memorable story can help set you apart hours later when the investor or recruiter is reflecting on everyone they saw that day.

Rebecca Fisher, the Director of the Drive Electric campaign, speaks regularly in pursuit of switching road transportation from fossil fuels to electric and I asked her about the power of storytelling in her advocacy. 'Whether it's speaking on a panel in front of hundreds of people or speaking one-on-one with a partner, I think what I've come to learn is that people don't want to hear about a jargony theory of change,' she said. 'They want to hear a story. The attention span of your audience is much better if you're leading them on a journey and making them feel things.'

Making people feel things: that's essential to why we're doing what we're doing. Of course we want to share a message, to enable some kind of change, but we all know deep down that the most effective change comes when we really *feel* something, rather than just know it on an intellectual level.

Sophie Williams, a speaker who specialises in the intersection of race, work and gender, thinks of it this way: 'My role as a speaker, as a storyteller, is to get that really dense information that can feel like it's behind a barrier, and to take away those barriers by turning those stats into things that don't feel one step removed, but that people can start to identify in their lives or the experiences of other people.' That's the power and magic of storytelling for me.

This is why I really advocate for using storytelling in your public speaking work. Throughout my years of experience in preparing people to speak, I've found that this has been a really effective approach in regards to imagining and writing the content they'll deliver. And remember: every time you speak, you are building on what you learned the previous time. The experts that you see giving great, memorable speeches, the kind you want to emulate, are not starting from scratch every time they have a speaking engagement. They're looking at their box of 'public speaking Lego' and figuring out which bits fit together in a pleasing way to create a finished product that serves their purpose and audience. If you're new to public speaking, you might want to start by getting an overview of what all the different elements can look like and learning what you're really trying to do with your storytelling. If you're a more experienced speaker, the 'assembly phase' of preparing your talk or presentation might be more about refining, casting your mind back to previous work and reflecting on whether you were playing to your strengths, or how you can take your presentation to the next level. In both cases it's about learning what your purpose is, what the purpose of this speaking opportunity is, and how you can create a speech based in storytelling that makes your audience feel empowered and motivated.

Stories don't have to be personal

When people think about 'storytelling', they often worry that it means they have to tell personal stories about themselves.

I've worked with speakers who use storytelling in a whole range of ways, and of course some, like the incredible Payzee Mahmod, base their storytelling around their own experiences, but many use storytelling without sharing a single fact of their own life. For example, I'm obsessed with Margaret Heffernan's TED talk, 'Forget the pecking order at work'. In it, she uses storytelling to bring to life research about productivity in chickens conducted by evolutionary biologist William Muir. It's a fascinating talk that makes ideas about organisational behaviour and productivity feel engaging and accessible, and uses storytelling to its full advantage.

Okay, so you've read all of this and maybe all this talk about the power and importance of storytelling has left you feeling a bit intimidated by the whole concept. But I want you to think about something: when was the last time you told a story? Whenever I ask people this, they often struggle to bring anything to mind. But I bet something embarrassing happened to you, or maybe you went on a bad date or saw something weird out of the bus window or had an awkward encounter at work – and you went away and told someone about it. And then maybe you told someone else, and when you told someone else, maybe you left out a detail that you realised wasn't relevant, or played up a moment that the first person reacted strongly to. Not only are you a storyteller, you're also already well aware of what makes a story compelling.

If the idea of storytelling still feels like something you'll never be able to access, the very wise public speaking coach

Simon Bucknall (who, if you ever see a book by him on speaking, you should absolutely buy) thinks of it like building up a level of fitness, not a one-time 'thing' you can either do or not do. 'Stories are a muscle you build over time. It's not as if you sit down for 10 minutes with a pad of A4 and a pen and suddenly you come up with a signature story that you then use for ten years. The best way to generate story ideas is through everyday conversations – where we tell stories all the time! Pay attention to the chats you have with friends, family and colleagues. These are a wonderful testbed for trying stuff out, to get a feel for which stories you actually enjoy.'

Stories are everywhere and all around you

I completely understand the feeling that you 'don't have' any stories to tell – this is something I hear a lot (and have often felt myself!). Comedian Sofie Hagen shared with me how they do it: 'I think of stories when I have a theme for a show, which is a tool people can use – but instead of a theme for a show, it can be a prompt. It's easy to think of a prompt, you can look at any book on your bookshelf or just look out the window: nature, change of seasons, camping, wildlife. It's what you do in conversations. Someone tells you about their favourite teacher, their most embarrassing date, a time they accidentally hurt someone – and stories from your own life come to mind. And, of course, there's the classic: What's the story you tell at parties?'

And if you think your line of work is too 'serious' for storytelling, can you imagine many situations more serious than presenting oral arguments to the US Supreme Court as a civil liberties lawyer? Esha Bhandari has done just that, and she told me she uses storytelling all the time. 'Every legal case has to have a story. It can't just be a set of legal doctrines that you say were violated. When you're speaking to judges, you're saying, *This is how the story should end, you should rule for me, so that the story can have this conclusion.* It's a huge part of how we frame cases, how we talk about legal doctrines.' Storytelling really can be powerful and useful in every situation, however high stakes or serious.

In contrast to the Planning phase, where I wanted you to follow each step in order and complete all five, the Assembly phase is more like a list of options – a toolbox, where you can use what you need, when you need it, rather than having to use everything all at once or in a specific order. There's no expectation that you'll use all of the ideas in this section, it's just a way of me offering up options that might help illuminate and improve your storytelling and public speaking. I encourage you to take from this part what makes you feel inspired and motivated, and to make choices that serve the message you're trying to share. If you try to do everything, you'll end up getting frustrated, whereas this is meant to be a fun, playful approach to storytelling.

How to begin

Human attention is a scarce commodity. We have more distractions than ever, more sources of information, more people making demands on our time and energy, more *things* that need to be done. When you're speaking to an audience of any kind or size, you're competing with their work to-do list, the desire to check their emails, even their curiosity about what they're going to have for dinner. You need to grab their attention – right from the start, with a strong opening.

It seems that while researchers can't quite agree on the precise number, it's safe to say that we make our minds up about our first impressions of a person within *seconds* of hearing them speak. You have to approach your talk, pitch, meeting or difficult conversation with the same mindset – that your opening is going to set the tone for how your audience perceives you throughout. The opening of your talk is the first building block in creating a rapport between you and your audience, however big or small it is.

Unless you've been explicitly told to, don't begin with 'Hi, my name is . . .' If you're onstage, don't even think about a nervous microphone tap and 'Um, can you all hear me?' – or the metaphorical equivalent in a smaller meeting. This is your time to shine! The moment you've been preparing for! It begins as soon as you walk on stage or sit down in front of a panel or simply as soon as you open your mouth to speak.

And, finally, I would advise that you don't open with a long preamble. It's okay to give a brief, concise and confident sign-posting of your speech, but starting with a rambly introduction full of disclaimers about your expertise or knowledge is giving your audience lots of opportunity to be distracted. It undermines your authority, and the audience won't necessarily differentiate it from the main body of your speech, so every single thing you go on to say will be seen through the same lens you made all of those disclaimers through. You don't need to apologise for yourself!

I've told you some ways *not* to begin a talk, but what about the things you *can* do? There are countless different ways to start, and it's up to you to figure out which one best serves the story you want to tell, the point you want to communicate, the impression you want to leave your audience with – whether that's a whole auditorium, or your boss when you are pitching for a raise. The opening you choose might also determine the rest of the structure of your talk, or offer a potential way of ending it, so keep your whole talk in mind when considering your opening.

To bring these techniques to life, I've sourced an example for each style so that you can see them in action by searching for the freely-available videos online.

Amplification: change the scale

This is actually one of my favourite ways of opening, which is why I'm addressing it first. The idea of Amplification as an opening technique is to change the perspective of the audience. That is to say, taking something complex and showing that it is simple – or vice versa. It challenges the listener's assumptions and so builds curiosity, and that's always a powerful way to keep someone listening. It can be about showing the audience a path forward, maybe in a way they hadn't considered before.

One way of thinking about Amplification is that it's about taking something small and making it big, or taking something big and making it small. Taking something that seems like a one-off moment and showing how it's directly connected to the bigger picture or problem, or taking something big and overwhelming and showing how it's manageable to tackle, that there's a way *into* it as a problem.

One example of this is when talking about climate change (something that I do a lot these days). For many people, climate change feels like this massive, incomprehensible and insurmountable problem. It can feel difficult and daunting for them to tackle, so they just don't engage. But if you bring that high-level big picture of climate change down to a smaller, core idea, like how you invest your money or how you heat your house, it doesn't seem quite so insurmountable or irrelevant to the individual. It isn't about minimising the issue, it's about giving people a way in that doesn't feel overwhelming, because when people get overwhelmed, they tend to freeze or shut down. Amplification can also work in the opposite direction, by taking something that feels so small and insignificant to the audience – like the temperature they have their thermostat set to – and demonstrating how such small things collectively contribute to climate change. Changing perspective, from big picture to close-up, or from close-up to big picture, can pique your audience's curiosity and hold their attention. Often this works by creating a sense of surprise in your listeners, which can also be a powerful tactic to lodge something in someone's memory. I find it's best if this opening is used to talk about a scenario that's *directly relevant* to your speech, rather than bringing in metaphors and analogies at this early point. So if you're talking about climate change and you want to open with Amplification, talk about climate change. Don't liken climate change to, I don't know, cooking or *The Lord of the Rings*.

One particularly memorable opening comes to mind when I think of Amplification. Sathya Raghu Mokkapati's talk at Aspen Ideas: Climate, 'Greenhouse-in-a-Box: Affordable Climate Tech', told the story of his encounter with a man in his village who he saw eating something off the ground. When he realised that the man was a farmer who was actually eating mud due to the lack of any other resources, it struck him as a powerful indictment of the impact that climate change has had on many of the millions of smallholder farmers in India. In this case, Sathya used Amplification to take something which at first appearances could be small or insignificant and used it as a way to open up or illustrate a much wider, far reaching issue.

Sensory: bring it to life

The idea of a Sensory introduction to your speech is about stimulating the imaginations of your audience by first stimulating their senses. This could be through sight, sound, smell, touch or taste, evoking memories or feelings in them that you can play on within your talk. This pokes at a primal part of our brains, playing on the most basic human sensory reactions.

And you don't have to create these sensations by asking the audience to smell, touch or taste real things. You can create those sensations with your words, because the human brain is not only capable of remembering sensations it's had before, but can conjure them up with no prior experience. You might not have been to, for example, a fish market in Tokyo, but I'm sure you can imagine the slippery floor underfoot, the sounds of traders, the smells of fish on ice, even the taste of silky, fatty raw tuna.

Maybe your speech involves discussing the place that you come from, which might be a place your audience has never been before. Asking the audience to close their eyes and imagine the bustling city you grew up in, the smells of the food being cooked on the street, the sound of the traffic, the feeling of the warm rain on your skin, the colour of the sky, the taste of a fruit that grows in your home country; all of that can help place them mentally in the location you want them to be in order for them to understand the point you want to make, the story you want to tell, about a change, a moment, a struggle that has occurred. You don't even have to use all five senses – just those that are useful to your story.

Beginning your speech with a Sensory opening can signal to the audience that you are a creative storyteller, someone they should listen to not just for the point you're making but also for the way you're telling it. Likewise, it's not for everyone, because the Sensory approach may not be relevant to your core message, and, as I mentioned before, the most important thing is to match the opening to the point you are trying to communicate, not show what a creative thinker you are. But this technique can be used to transport the listener to another place, and makes for a really powerful opening when combined with a strong opening story.

In his TED talk 'The Anti-CEO Playbook', Hamdi Ulukaya, the CEO of yoghurt brand Chobani, gives a really evocative description of his first encounter with the disused yoghurt plant that would completely change his life. You get a sense of the fateful drive to the plant, the first smells (not pleasant!), the texture of the walls, the stories contained within the factory contrasting with the silence that he heard when he visited, the weight of the history of the place. It gives you an understanding of not just the situation Hamdi is describing, but how those sensory experiences affected him, and, most importantly, *why* they relate to the theme of his talk, which is around being an 'anti-CEO'. It gives you a perspective on his experience that allows you to feel like you were right there with him, sitting next to him in the car on the way to the factory, and the state of mind he might have had when he made these life-changing decisions.

Personalisation: make it relevant

Let's face it, people like to focus on themselves. Whether it's someone monologuing to you at a party, or that friend who can't help themselves from hearing an anecdote and then immediately relating it back to themselves. It's a human impulse! And you can play on that to your advantage in public speaking by making your audience feel like the centre of the story. By turning *your* world into *their* world.

It's about taking something that they know on an intellectual level to be true, of concern or of importance to other people, and making it *feel* true on an emotional level. You want them to listen to your talk with the feeling of being personally invested in the point you're trying to communicate, whether by confronting them with the fact that the problem could affect them, or that they could be in a position to resolve the problem.

I've heard some amazing talks on disability that felt as if they really got to the heart of this. Disability is something that, for many reasons including cultural prejudice and a refusal to believe it could happen to them, people want to distance themselves from. Both Stella Young and Sophie Morgan's TEDx talks do an amazing job of bridging the gap between disabled and non-disabled people and trying to communicate the realities of navigating the world as a disabled person. Stella's is called 'I'm not your inspiration, thank you very much', and it's a funny, subversive take on the experience of being inherently 'inspirational' as a disabled person, however irrelevant and/or patronising that might be. Sophie's is titled 'Air travel is failing disabled people – here's the truth', and details the ways that flying strips disabled people and especially wheelchair users of their dignity.

Ash Beckham's TED talk, meanwhile, 'We're all hiding something', makes the personal – the idea of 'coming out of the closet' – feel universal by encouraging the audience to think about the experiences they've had with the same dynamic, even if it's different from Ash's. She reclaims the idea of 'the closet' from just being the typical understanding of 'coming out' as LGBTQIA+, and reframes it as any difficult conversation, such as telling someone you have cancer or saying 'I love you' for the first time. In Ash's case, it was questions from strangers about her gender, but she creates room within the talk for the audience to understand 'coming out of the closet' in relation to their own experiences. This hopefully allows the talk to feel universal and gets every audience member thinking about what the speaker's words mean to them, and, likewise, prevents them from switching off because they think it's not relevant to them.

A Personalisation opening isn't necessarily about sharing personal or intimate information with your audience. You don't need to make that part of your story. Instead, it's about getting the audience to understand your core message on a personal level, rather than an intellectual one, in the hope that by connecting the message directly to the audience, they're more likely to stay engaged with what you have to say throughout your speech.

False Start: surprise them

A False Start structure is exactly what it sounds like! It's a little bit of misdirection for the audience, lulling them into a false sense of security that they know what's going on and then bam! You hit them with a change of direction. What's key to this structure is that it's about disrupting the predictable. You want to be telling the kind of story that the audience *thinks* they already know. As with so many of these storytelling approaches, the power is in the contrast, the subversion, the disruption. So, for once, it's kind of okay to be telling a pretty predictable and pedestrian story, or at least something the audience will recognise as such without them using too much brain power, because the whole point of the False Start is that you don't let that part drag on too long before taking that swerve in a different direction.

Stefanie Reid's TEDxLondonWomen talk, 'Why accessible design is for everyone', does just this. She sets up what seems like it's going to be a familiar structure: beginning on her thirty-second birthday, she reflects that on that date she had spent the same amount of time being disabled as she had been able-bodied. She goes on to say it allowed her to see what the difference was between Stef as an able-bodied person and Stef as a disabled person, so the audience is expecting the rest of the talk to be a deep dive into those differences as a way we can learn about accessible design. But nope! False Start! Instead, she surprises the audience by saying that she learned the difference between the two 'versions' of Stef was, in fact, 'not very much'.

And all this happens within the space of one minute. The talk sets and then re-sets our expectations in less than sixty seconds. That's the kind of scale you want to be working with, so the audience doesn't settle into the pedestrian and predictable style of storytelling too willingly. You've got to keep them on their toes, right?

Something that makes Stef's talk even more effective is that, after the False Start, she goes on to detail assumptions she herself made, and then the ways in which real life subverted those assumptions, which mirrors the overall structure of the story.

This could be an effective approach to use if there's a moment in *your* story where *you* had essentially been lulled into a false sense of security or complacency, going along with the status quo, before something happened – whether that's an inciting incident or just a philosophical realisation or change of heart – that made you swerve in a different direction, just like you're doing with the audience. It implicitly encourages flexible thinking, being open to new ideas and changing your mind about things, which is exactly what you're trying to do with your talk or presentation or conversation. For example, if you studied clothing design and thought you knew how to design clothes for 'all shapes and sizes' before taking a job at a plus-size brand, and then realised you'd actually been making samples in the same small size the whole time before expanding your understanding of what 'all shapes and sizes' really means.

Puzzle: make them think

Who's the best-selling novelist of all time? Harry Potter has sold a tonne of copies, right? Maybe Stephen King? He's been going a long time, written a lot of books. It's not Stephen King, though. It's Agatha Christie. Because we *love* a mystery. We love being presented with something impossible, something brain-teasing, something curiosity-spiking, and trying our hardest to work out how it's done. It doesn't matter how old we are: we love a puzzle.

Not only do puzzles appeal to our natural curiosity, it also adds a personalisation element: the audience wants to solve the puzzle and figure out the answer – they are invested. This is what makes it a potentially great opening. You're hooking the audience from the very beginning by posing a question or making a statement that they *want* to engage with.

If you choose to begin with a Puzzle opening, you can either make it directly and literally relevant to the subject of your talk, or it can be more cryptic and metaphorical. Likewise, you can either give the solution after a brief pause to let the audience think about the answer, or you can leave them hanging until the very end. Though while it can be tempting to leave them hanging for dramatic effect, you have to make sure that the content of your speech is engaging enough that their mind won't be wandering to your mystery, and that the reveal at the end is sufficiently satisfying so they will be leaving on a high, rather than a 'huh?!'

Think of a fundamental paradox in your field of knowledge that's relevant to your talk. Is there a way that you can turn this into a Puzzle to give yourself that engaging opening? If so, then maybe this opening style is the one for you!

A great example of this is the psychotherapist and broadcaster Philippa Perry's RSA talk, 'Parenting Tips with Philippa Perry'. In it, she recounts an experience of her father overhearing her tell another adult that she wasn't having a particularly happy childhood, which sparked a tirade from him: '. . . he came over, he shouted at me, "you're having an idyllic childhood, a brilliant childhood, how can you say that, stupid girl!"' Philippa Perry goes on to explain the paradox that we want our children to be happy so much that we try to scold them into being happy. This paradox forms the basis of her unpicking a better way to relate to our children during her talk.

Question: make them wonder

Lots of people like the idea of using a question to open a talk or presentation and it can seem like a simple option. But it can be surprisingly hard to do well! It's kind of like the Puzzle opener, but without that extra layer of curiosity or paradox.

It sounds simple: just open with a question.

This could feel like an accessible way to start your talk, especially given how many *kinds* of questions there are. I suggest never asking a closed question (i.e. one which, generally, has one specific yes or no answer, or a single factual response). Instead, it's better to use something more open – where the listener can explore an answer in their heads, and not think you're expecting a specific reply, even if they might have some ideas.

For example, when I was working with journalist and TEDxLondonWomen speaker Sahar Zand, she wanted to talk about her childhood in Iran and the impact of her gender on her experience of growing up. So she started by asking the audience a seemingly simple question: 'When you were a child, what did you want to be when you grew up?' These kinds of questions are used for dramatic effect more than in pursuit of an answer. Your aim is to get the listener to be thinking about what you need them to – to get them into the right mindset to receive the rest of what you'll be saying. Because it's already slightly abstract, it's important to make it clear that the question you're asking *is* directly related to your talk, even if at first glance it appears not to be. You can go on to do that in the main body of your speech, or even right at the end – as long as the connection becomes obvious to the audience. Watch Sahar's talk, 'Why Iranians are cutting their hair for "Woman, Life, Freedom" ', to see how she uses her surprising answer to bring to life the experience of millions of women and girls in Iran.

Now, I know I just made it all seem really straightforward, but the problem is, it's not; there are lots of ways a question can go wrong. If you simply choose the wrong question, it can fall flat with the audience and leave them feeling baffled and distracted. It's also really important not to use knowledge-based questions, however obvious the answer might seem (Richard Osman, former co-host of the TV quiz show *Pointless*, once cited a round of the show where only 91 out of 100 people could identify a picture of a blue and green planet beginning with E as 'earth', so you really can't rely on 100 per cent of people having the answer to *any* question). Likewise, *did you know that* . . . is often a bad way to start a question, whether the answer is yes or no. If yes, then it takes away a little bit of your authority, and if no, it can leave the audience feeling uncomfortable that they didn't have the knowledge they should have had. This might leave you thinking a rhetorical question is the solution, but it's important to make sure it doesn't feel patronising. Another pitfall to avoid are questions or ways of asking rhetorical questions that have become clichéd. Two that immediately come to mind when I'm working with TED and TEDx speakers are: *Did you know that . . .* and *What if I told you that . . .* There is nothing inherently wrong with asking questions in this way, but, unfortunately, these approaches have just been used too many times to have the impact that, as a speaker, you would want them to.

This isn't necessarily to put you off using questions, it's more to make you think carefully. It's about starting to really whittle your question down to what you can ask in a way that stimulates your listeners' inner world. What is the question that gets the audience to think about what you want them to without losing them in the depths of that inner world?

One example of an opening using a question to do this really well is Rachel Botsman's TED talk 'The currency of the new economy is trust', which she begins by asking the audience which three words sum up your reputation. This sets the tone for the rest of the talk and gives a framework for the audience to understand it. Maybe more importantly, asking a question *to* the audience *about* the audience means they are more likely to see how this talk relates to them personally, and it helps them to engage with it in a more meaningful way. It's also a question that doesn't have one fixed answer, doesn't assume knowledge and doesn't feel patronising. It's a perfect question in that respect!

If you want to begin with the Question opening, try to think of it in relation to your core message. What is the best question I could ask that would get the audience thinking about my one main idea?

If you're trying to work on your networking skills, what are some questions you can have ready to ask when you're in those one-to-one situations? Earlier in my career I got to work with former hostage negotiator turned communications expert Richard Mullender, and one question he told me he really likes to ask is 'how do you spend most of your time?', which allows someone to answer in a way that allows them to talk about their passions, whether or not that's their work. Other go-to questions for me are 'what brought you here today?' or 'has anything exciting happened to you today?'

Narrative: tell a story

Given how passionate I am about storytelling and its uses in public speaking, it's maybe not that surprising that I consider a story a good way to open. You already know how I feel about stories and narratives – they're brain-stimulating, they're a way to forge human connections, make sense of the world, etc etc – so I won't go over it again. There are so many different approaches to 'story' that you could take for your opening, whether that's a well-known fable that either perfectly illustrates your point *or* you want to subvert during your talk, or maybe a story from your own life and own experiences that the audience won't have heard before because it's yours.

Fenhinti Balogun opened his talk at TED Countdown, 'How to find your voice for climate action', with a really powerful story of how he could not fully engage with an exciting moment in his acting career because of climate change and the anxiety it left him with. It gave an insight into how serious this topic felt for him as a speaker, and created a captivating opening to his talk.

I also think of Margaret Heffernan's talk 'Forget the pecking order at work', which she opened with a story about the behaviour of chickens to illustrate the point of her talk. This also shows that 'stories' don't need to be personal to work: if you choose a clear example that is relevant to the rest of the talk, it can basically be about anything, even chicken research!

Don't overlook and undervalue your own experiences when thinking about what constitutes a 'story'. Expert speaker and coach Simon Bucknall (and my co-host on the podcast *Speechless*), recommends taking stock of your life experience and thinking about whether there are any stories there that will help you illustrate what you're trying to say. 'The key is to switch off the editor,' he said. Ask yourself: 'What are the moments that I remember? You could pick a chapter of your life. It could be the last week, the last year. It could be childhood, it could be school, it could be your first job, whatever it is. Get specific and just start chucking jelly at the wall. But don't worry about whether you'll use the story or how you'll use it. That decision can come later.'

As with all opening styles, Tell A Story should feel integrated into the overall project of your talk rather than disconnected. This means that, if you open with a story, it should feel like a natural beginning to the rest of your speech. Maybe that means it's got imagery you return to throughout the talk, or you borrow the structure of your speech from the story, or it's an anecdote from your life that explains how you reached the conclusion that you want to share with your audience. Another fun way to play on your opening story is to tell a story that everyone thinks they know the ending to, but by the end of your talk or presentation or conversation, you conclude it by surprising them with a different ending altogether.

Oh and, regarding humour, if it's important that the story's funny, make sure the story is actually funny! And more than that, make sure it's appropriate to the audience you're speaking to. There will be nothing worse for your confidence than assuming your humour will land with the audience and then . . . crickets. The opening is a high-stakes moment, as it will set the tone for how you feel throughout the rest of your time in the spotlight, so don't do anything to knock yourself off-balance if you can help it!

How to choose?

Please remember: these openings are supposed to inspire you, not limit you. You can always mix and match bits from different opening styles and come up with something that feels uniquely *you*.

I give you these examples not to make you feel constrained by them, or that your opening needs to neatly fit into a box. Instead, I want you to think creatively about all the options you have at your disposal to draw the audience in at the most important moment. Making choices in service of your audience and your message is the most important thing.

When deciding which of these openings you would like to try, think about the following five questions:

- Who is my audience?
- What style(s) might fit the context best? Is this a formal talk, an interview, a presentation or a conversation?
- Which one or two openings am I most excited by or feel most like me?
- Does my core message or idea lend itself more easily to one or more techniques?
- What ideas, stories, data etc do I have that I could use?

This first question can be tricky, because sometimes you don't know a lot about who you're speaking to. Or they might be very diverse and you're not sure if there is one way to speak to all of them. In this case, using curiosity as your guiding principle can be very helpful – it is an almost universal currency.

Curiosity starts as this little kick in the reward centre of the brain, and if you make people curious, it's inevitable they'll want to know more, want to keep listening, will wait for you to spill the beans. They can't help it!

Returning to the work of the economist and psychologist George Loewenstein, he suggests that the function of curiosity is to *motivate* learning, and he coined the idea of the 'information gap' – you know the information is out there but you don't have it yet. Imagine you're walking behind someone on the street, you can see the back of their head and the clothes they're wearing, but you get really invested in knowing what their face looks like. Even though knowing what they look like doesn't impact you in any way – your mind wants to fill that gap in your knowledge.

Think of your opening as the way to create the information gap for your listeners, and let the content and ideas you have to share *inform* how you approach creating that gap. You can provoke the audience's curiosity using any of the openings I've detailed here, not just the more 'intriguing' ones, like the Question or Puzzle.

Try thinking about your content in the following ways, and the right way to begin should hopefully present itself to you:

- Is there a question you can ask to get the audience thinking about your core idea and themselves?
- Can you describe a gap in your audience's knowledge that your talk is going to fill in?
- Is there a story or anecdote about your core idea you can share that will surprise or delight your audience?

How to structure your story

So you know the story that you want to tell, the perfect anecdote to illustrate your point, or the ideal way to communicate your big idea via storytelling. But you don't know *how* to tell the story. You know what the point is, but when you tell the story, you find your listeners miss that point, or you don't quite convey why it's important. I'm going to share with you lots of different ways to structure stories, and hopefully one of those will speak to you and help you bring your material to life and help you animate your ideas via storytelling. Again, try to remember that you can use these approaches and structures in two ways: one is to structure the stories themselves that you use *within* talks, conversations and presentations, and the other is to structure the overall flow of the talk.

Cognitive economist Leigh Caldwell told me that 'the nature of good storytelling ties very deeply into that basic cause-and-effect learning that is probably the most powerful, fundamental tool that the brain has for mastering the world around it. That means both that good storytelling emerges naturally from the way the brain learns, but also that by doing good storytelling, you can communicate and teach people cause and effect in a very effective way. It's a very natural way to get people to learn things from you, or to influence people's behaviour, because you're tapping into the way that their brains naturally want to learn.' It's important to never forget that idea of cause and effect when it comes to structuring a story that you want to work as a story on its own terms.

The creators of South Park, Matt Stone and Trey Parker, have a pretty simple way to think about writing a compelling story. They shared it in a writing seminar at NYU in 2014, which you can watch online, but here's the nugget of wisdom that I really loved from that seminar: 'We can take these beats, which are basically the beats of your outline, and if the words "and then" belong between those beats, you're fucked, basically, you got something pretty boring. What should happen between every beat that you've written down is either the word "therefore" or "but".' Otherwise you just have a list of things, but that's not a story.

Let the story lead the way

When you think about the story you want to tell or the idea you want to share, that story or idea may inherently suggest the best structure required to tell it. David Biello, the award-winning science journalist and TED's climate curator, explained it to me like this: 'Storytelling is important, but it's also important to have an idea, a point, a moral, whatever it might be, to inform that storytelling, because it also informs the choices you're going to make in the way you tell that story. You could tell Little Red Riding Hood in any number of ways. You could tell it from the point of view of the wolf. You can tell it from some omniscient narrator point of view, but the point that you're trying to make is going to tell you how to tell that story.'

Something worth noting is that although all of these are great storytelling structures, there are a few that, by their nature, are better-suited to longer formats. The Mountain Range, Sparklines, Petals and Nested Loops approaches featured in upcoming sections are good ways to arrange and communicate larger amounts of information, for example, and don't work quite as well if you're dealing with shorter time frames or less information-dense content. On the other hand, Story Sandwich, Problem-Solution and the Pixar Pitch are really good in situations where you need to be more concise, like a panel or a Q&A, but still have something important you want to share with the audience. There are a couple – Petals and Converging Ideas – that I think suit situations where more than one person is presenting, so I've saved those for the end. With that in mind, let's dig into structure . . .

Story Sandwich

Not that I'm always thinking in terms of food analogies, but I like to think of this structure as the Story Sandwich. You've got two pieces of bread: the first slice is your point. Your core message. Remember that from way back at the beginning of the book? Don't lose sight of that now we're thinking about stories! Right, so, your core message goes first. Then the filling of the sandwich is a delicious story. Then, after the filling, there's the bread again, which means you restate, and bring everything back to, your core message. See how that makes a sandwich?

> A conversation I like to use to illustrate this kind of approach is Hal Harvey and John Doerr's 'How to decarbonize the grid and electrify everything'. They open by talking about the problems of relying on carbon to power energy grids, and the urgent need to electrify them instead, taking us through why this is a pressing issue, making sure we understand that the solution is electrification. After laying out the key issues, John Doerr literally signals to Hal Harvey and to the

> audience (us) that *he is going to tell us a story*. It's as simple as that. You don't even need to be subtle about it! You can come right out and say it, and the audience will come along with you.

Of course, it's important that the story you choose is actually meaningful and contributes to the audience's understanding of your core message. It can't just be any old story. We want to be choosing a story that brings your message to life.

The way it slightly deviates from being an actual Sandwich is that, when you bring it back to the 'point' after the story, you can't just say exactly the same stuff you said at the beginning. It isn't actually a question of two identical slices of bread. The key to making this a good structure for storytelling and giving compelling talks and presentations is by adding that something extra at the end. It's restating your overall point *plus a little bit extra*. Maybe that extra thing is a proposed solution, maybe it's examples of where this problem has been successfully addressed in the past, maybe it's the facts and figures that prove that the approach you're proposing is the right one. It's staying on track with your core message, but sprinkling that extra something on top. Think of it like a conclusion to an essay in that way: you don't copy and paste the same things you said in the introduction, but you don't necessarily want to bring in whole new *ideas* here either. It's about going that bit deeper on your 'point' because the audience now has the foundation of the 'story' you just shared in the middle of the Sandwich.

One of the reasons why this structure works is because, if you tell people your big idea and then tell a story, people can forget the big idea by the time they've heard the story. Reminding them of the big idea again at the end reinforces the message you're trying to share. If you think about the situation you're in, like a panel or a meeting or a conference, it's important to speak very concisely and get your point across, and this can be a great way to do that.

Problem-Solution

Usually, your objective in giving a talk is to bring about some kind of change. That probably means you're not entirely happy with the way things are now. In other words, there's a problem.

One of the most natural ways for people to respond when presented with a problem is to want to find a way to solve it (the other is to deny that it's really a problem). And you can take advantage of this by structuring your talk in a relatively simple way: talk about the problem, and then present a possible solution.

This can be a really compelling way to lay out your story, and one that a lot of speakers I know use. It can also be a great way to help people see that change is possible and get them to imagine a different way of doing things.

So this story structure is pretty simple: you present the problem, and then you present the solution. But there's something really important that goes in between those two points. In order for both your problem and your solution to resonate with the audience, you have to do the work to make the problem feel real to them. Make sure you're building all the important information into your narrative so that the listeners feel invested and all fired up to help you change things.

> Vidhya Ramalingam, founder of Moonshot, uses storytelling in her work, where she uses technology to disrupt and counter online harms. She knows that you can't shy away from difficult issues, but proposes always pairing problems with solutions. Vidhya told me about the way she structures storytelling in her work, and although different approaches will work for everyone, I wanted to include her strategy for how to structure a story here, in her own words:
>
> I always start with building credibility, so that they know why they should be listening to me – not going through your entire bio, but just drop in one line on one thing you've done that establishes credibility.
>
> Next is introduce the problem, and always add a bit of emotional, personal pull to the problem, so that it doesn't just feel like something people read in the news, but it feels personal to them or something they can empathise with.
>
> And then, once you've talked through the problem, you move into optimism. You want them to understand *this is awful, but hang on a second, we can do something about this*. And then take them through what can we do about it? What is the solution?

> When I describe the solution, I always give an example of the solution in practice, where something was solved, where a life was saved, or where someone who was thinking of doing something violent went on a different path. So that it's really clear, this isn't just a hope and a dream. No, this actually works. It's based on evidence, it's happening around us all the time. With the idea being that you never introduce a problem without giving that optimistic solution. But it's not just hopeful optimism, it's evidence-based optimism because we know that we can do something about it.

All this can form a really useful framework for stories you want to tell with a Problem-Solution structure, and I especially like the idea of evidence-based optimism: you want to leave your audience feeling genuinely empowered to help you enact change, rather than just nebulously inspired.

If you do go down the Problem-Solution route, it's important to remember two things. Firstly, the problem can't be so overwhelming that people feel as if no solution will ever work, but it can't be so small that your audience doesn't care about it. Secondly, the problem and the solution have to 'match' in terms of scale. For example, you can't tell the audience that we're on the brink of catastrophic climate change that will affect every single person on the planet and cost billions of lives, and then tell them the solution is ending plastic straws. It's mismatched. Imagine an old-fashioned scale: whatever you put on the 'problem' side has to be heavy enough to weigh it down, but not so heavy that nothing you put on the 'solution' side could possibly match it.

The Hero's Journey

Sometimes it's nice to have a tried and tested structure to rely on. Enter The Hero's Journey.

It's a tale as old as time, but it works for a reason. If you're not familiar with The Hero's Journey, it's *the* way of structuring narratives, the mother of all story structures, also known as the 'monomyth'. People have been telling stories in this structure since time immemorial, but its distinct phases or 'beats' were codified and popularised by Joseph Campbell in 1949, and then updated by Christopher Vogler in 2007 to reflect contemporary storytelling conventions. Think about the last blockbuster you saw. It probably had a structure that went a bit like this: First, we meet the hero in their ordinary world. Then they receive a call to adventure, which initially they reject. They then accept the call, and soon meet a 'mentor' figure who will guide them through this adventure. They cross the first 'threshold' into the new world, which begins Act Two of the story. In Act Two, they will face tests, and both allies and enemies, before they approach the 'inmost cave' where the real challenge lies. They undergo an ordeal that leads them to receive a physical or metaphorical reward. End of Act Two! In Act Three, they wrap things up by taking the road back home, experience a kind of resurrection, and return with 'the elixir'. If you follow Joseph Campbell and Christopher Vogler, that is the 'One Story to Rule Them All'. Now, while I am a fan of many different kinds of story structure, that really is a good one. If it's good enough for everything from *Moby-Dick* to *The Lord of the Rings*, *Star Wars* to Homer's *Odyssey*, you can see how versatile The Hero's Journey is.

Amid the multiple beats in the story structure, it's really important not to lose sight of what The Hero's Journey is fundamentally *about*. It's about change, and more specifically about the protagonist of the story being changed. At its core, The Hero's Journey is about a hero who goes on an adventure, faces challenges and, in a decisive crisis, wins a victory. The hero then returns home changed or transformed. The change, the transformation, is at the heart of *all* stories, whether they follow this specific structure or not, so even if you don't use The Hero's Journey structure, try to always be identifying that point of transformation in your story.

Have a think about the key 'elements' or 'points' of your story. Can you see ways that these points hit the key beats of The Hero's Journey? It may not be immediately obvious to you, but if it's a story about how you came up against a challenge and overcame it, odds are you can take your story and break it down into these parts. A TED talk you can use for inspiration is BLACK's 2013 talk, 'My journey to yo-yo mastery'. Yep, you read that right, it's about yo-yos! The Japanese yo-yo master BLACK uses The Hero's Journey structure to document his progress from where he started to where he's ended up today. Spoiler: he's pretty great at yo-yoing.

Do remember, though, that just because this structure can be applied to almost any story, it doesn't necessarily mean that it's the right structure for *every* story. It's definitely not one-size-fits all, so make sure it's the right choice for you and your message.

The Heroine's Journey

The Hero's Journey is a classic for a reason, but it's not without its potential pitfalls. I spoke to the brilliant filmmaker and storyteller Matt Golding, and he spoke about The Hero's Journey from a critical perspective I hadn't considered before. 'We have quite an extractive, hierarchical, violent storytelling framework in The Hero's Journey,' he told me. 'When you look at how often some of those stories came from myths and legends, they're often stories of wars and battles. Our son was given the Golden Fleece story recently, and in the first page of the book, a group is trying to steal a magical Golden Fleece. The goal is theft, and everything spans from that, so your Hero's Journey is built around the idea that you're going to steal something from another community who are going to suffer its loss. That's like a classic story arc of our culture. It's not surprising that we have built an extractive society when we tell each other extractive stories. So I think we have a responsibility as storytellers to acknowledge that and change it.'

Now, Matt is thinking about the possibilities of storytelling in particularly deep and radical ways, but it's something that might benefit us all to consider. Matt signposted me towards an alternative model: The Heroine's Journey, originated by Maureen Murdock in her book (published in 1990) of the same name. 'This is much more useful in terms of telling stories of social change, because the whole point of it is it tells stories where somebody provokes something that is unusual or counter to the dominant social norm, and then over time, they go on a journey that flips the social norm of the society they're in.'

So while there are similarities with the structure, The Heroine's Journey takes a more expansive approach. Rather than one single warrior forging their path through the world as it is, this is about reflecting on how the protagonist can change the world, rather than themselves. If you want to learn more about this idea, have a look at the Maureen Murdock book, or at Kim Hudson's book *The Virgin's Promise* (2009), which takes its own approach to storytelling.

Kishotenketsu

If there is no inherent conflict in the subject of your talk, you might find yourself trying to create some strife just to give the story more structure and drive it forward. But maybe you don't want to have to invent an enemy just to tell your personal story in a job interview, say, or simply present your KPIs to the management team.

It turns out the need for conflict to drive a story is associated much more with the Western narrative tradition than with stories from other parts of the world. One notable alternative structure, originating in Chinese poetry, and adopted in Japanese and Korean media too, is *Kishotenketsu*.

In this structure, a story has four parts: *ki*, *sho*, *ten* and *ketsu* – which together give the structure its name.

Ki, or 'setup', is where the story is introduced. Typically we meet the characters and learn the context in which they live.

Sho, or 'development', provides more details and expands on the situation. Unlike in The Hero's Journey or a three-act structure, there is no requirement for conflict – the characters may not have an enemy or even an identifiable need or objective.

Ten, usually translated as 'twist', changes how we see the situation. This might be through the introduction of a new character with their own, different, perspective. It could be an event that presents a dilemma to the characters. Or you might simply invite the listener to see the situation in a new way. Sometimes this revelation can even change the genre of the story, for instance with the introduction of a crime or a magical element. If you do want to include a conflict in the story, it can be introduced at this stage.

The final stage, *ketsu* or 'conclusion', plays out the impact of the twist; but not necessarily in a neat resolution that solves the problem. The *ketsu* often unites the new perspective (revealed by the twist) with the world presented in the first two stages. This is sometimes called reconciliation, and can provide a satisfying end to the story, but it does not necessarily mean that the protagonist got what they wanted.

As there is no conflict (necessarily) in *Kishotenketsu*, there is no need for a conflict to be resolved in its final stage. This form can be used to leave a question asked but not answered, or to allow the audience more freedom to decide their own attitude to the events portrayed. In the poetic form from which this structure comes, the fourth line is described as allowing the reader to reflect on the meaning of the whole poem.

The films *Parasite* and *My Neighbour Totoro* follow this structure, and it is often seen in Japanese manga comics. One popular form of short comic strip, *yonkoma*, encapsulates each of the four stages in a single panel.

Many of the speaking opportunities and topics you are likely to encounter do not contain a conflict that needs discussing or resolving. Instead, you may want to present an existing world in some detail, introduce a different perspective, then integrate the two views into a new synthesis. I see *Kishotenketsu* as a natural fit for these talks.

Pixar Pitch

Are you ready to have your mind blown? All Pixar movies follow this six-point structure:

- Once upon a time . . .
- Every day . . .
- then one day . . .
- Because of that . . .
- Because of that . . .
- Until, finally . . .

We call it the Pixar Pitch, but it seems that an improv teacher called Kenn Adams was actually the first person to formalise this way of breaking down a narrative into its parts, and you can apply this formula to your story too. It has a beginning, middle and end, which replicates the classic three-act structure that also appears in The Hero's Journey. In a way, the Pixar Pitch (also known as the Story Spine) is actually just a streamlined, pithier version of The Hero's Journey. As a speaker, you can use this structure as a six-point checklist. It gets you to ask the right questions, like are you starting at the right place? Does your turning point come in a logical place in the story? Is your protagonist the right protagonist? Are the consequences the right consequences? Are you ending where you want to end? Speakers often start in the wrong place, or their turning point will focus on the wrong thing, but they can't quite see why their story isn't landing. The Pixar Pitch is a neat and clear way to determine a structure for the story you're trying to tell. If you think of the 'And then one day' as the moment in the Pixar movie that changes everything, ask yourself what that would look like in your own story. You might find it useful to start with the third sentence and work back and forward from there. What was the 'And then one day' of your story? What was life like before that moment? And how did that moment change the course of your story to lead you to where you are today, knowing what you know and doing what you do?

No matter how technical or complicated your idea or story is, the Pixar Pitch approach shows that nothing is too complex to be boiled down to something simple. Yes, it's kind of a stripped-back version of The Hero's Journey in some ways, except it gets you to think in a more intentional and focused way about the *consequences* of things that are happening in the story. Things don't just happen in isolation, they are caused by and lead to other things.

This structure works well when moving the audience through your personal or organisational story so far. Following the Pixar Pitch structure can allow you to move through contextual information in a streamlined way by keeping it focused on *consequences*. It's not about including as much information as possible, it's about focusing on these six key points of your narrative. These are the essential moments that *had* to happen to propel you to the ending, where you speak from today.

Have a think about how you could tell your story using this structure. Here's an example I could use from my own life that tells the story of how and why I ended up being a speaker coach:

1. (Once upon a time . . .) *I worked at a small human rights charity in London.*
2. (Every day . . .) *I saw us fail to reach the people and institutions we needed to influence to stop real people suffering.*
3. (One day . . .) *in 2011, I was invited to a livestream of the first ever TEDWomen conference. I was in awe. I started to see the power of storytelling to create impact.*
4. (Because of that . . .) *I ran my first TEDx event later that year with 100 people, bad lighting and a stage set made up of random objects from my living room – it was wonderful!*
5. (Because of that . . .) *I made it my mission to keep supporting voices and ideas that needed to be heard.*
6. (Until finally . . .) *a decade later, I run one of the world's top TEDx events, have worked with hundreds of speakers who have been heard by tens of millions of people and who have changed the law in England and Wales to protect children and have raised over $1 billion to fight climate change.*

The Mountain Range

Think about it: when most people speak, maybe telling an anecdote in everyday conversation or recounting a recent experience they've had, it's with a vaguely linear, slightly rambling structure that *might* get to the 'point' at around the 80 per cent mark, but doesn't really, structurally speaking, do much along the way. They're doing some freeform meandering, maybe straying from the path a little bit. If you want people to keep listening, this really isn't a great plan. Instead, you want to be leading your listeners to the conclusion, and one way of doing that is the Mountain Range.

With the Mountain Range approach, instead of meandering along a path and hoping your audience comes along for the ride, think of yourself as the hiking guide for a group of walkers (your audience). Your job is to take them up and down a series of peaks and descents until you reach the Big One, the Matterhorn, the Everest, of your single idea.

This means adding in moments along the way – those smaller mountain peaks – that really build your narrative while incorporating the kind of tonal variety that keeps the audience engaged. That's the key to this structure, the up and down, the back and forth. I like to think of these mini peaks as 'aha!' moments: they're smaller chunks of the storytelling that deliver insight or information so that you're continuously hooking the audience in until they get to the final conclusion. You could think of those peaks as the preparation you need to get the audience in the right headspace or knowledge base to digest your overarching message, just like hiking up a smaller mountain would give someone the confidence to tackle something bigger.

But it's not just about how you reach that final, biggest summit: in the spirit of thinking of yourself as a hiking guide, you wouldn't leave your group at the top of the highest mountain. Part of the work is necessarily about bringing your audience back *down* the other side with you. It's still important to find an elegant way to end, to neatly wrap up the content and bring it all together, rather than just ending at this huge, final peak with the audience completely overwhelmed and bewildered!

The Mountain Range is a great approach to take when you're dealing with longer-form content that *needs* to be presented sequentially. It's about pacing and creating tonal variety within a talk or presentation that already has a predetermined chronology or timeline or order that you're laying out. Melinda Janki's 'How we took on an oil giant—and won' is a great example: she uses the Mountain Range to lead the audience through her account of battling ExxonMobil and their activity in her home country of Guyana. Sometimes she experiences success, sometimes she experiences setbacks (which helps create the peaks and valleys of the metaphorical Mountain Range), but ultimately she is guiding you through a story that has a set order.

In Medias Res

Record scratch – freeze frame – *You're probably wondering how I got into this mess*. Sound familiar? If you've ever seen a film or a TV show that started like this, then you already know how an *In Medias Res* approach to storytelling works.

Put simply, the way of telling a story *In Medias Res* is by starting the story at the height of the action and then jumping back to the beginning, rather than starting at the beginning of the story the way you normally would.

The reason it has a Latin name is that this storytelling technique goes *way* back, and not to say that all old things are inherently good, but there's a reason it's been an enduring storytelling style for literally thousands of years. One of the most iconic examples of *In Medias Res* is the *Odyssey*, the epic poem by Homer, which begins with Odysseus's journey home from the Trojan war, with flashbacks and storytelling to fill in the past.

One of the downsides to this approach is that it can initially be bewildering for the audience, who has no idea what's going on. Obviously, that's intrinsic to the way the storytelling style works, but it just means that it's really important that everything *else* you're doing is clear and coherent, and you're not forgetting to include important details that will make the jump-start easier to follow for the people listening. Likewise, just because the audience knows how things turn out, because you've already given them the middle of the story, don't neglect all the fundamental beats that led you to that point. Make sure the actual story works on its own merit, without relying on the context of the flashback structure to fill in the gaps.

If you want an example of an amazing talk that uses an *In Medias Res* opening, then check out Zak Ebrahim's TED talk 'I am the son of a terrorist. Here's how I chose peace', which, at the time of writing, has been watched on the TED platform alone nearly seven million times, for good reason. He begins with the story of one man walking into a hotel in Manhattan to murder another, which is a pretty compelling way to open. Of course, he gives you the context, his connection to the incident and the implications for what he wants to talk about in the fullness of time, but it's such a striking opening that the audience can't help but hold their breath and wait to find out more. It also works because it's clear. It's a really straightforward story, even if the ideas Zak wants to deal with are complex and emotionally-charged.

This could be a great structure to use if there's a moment in your story that's obviously *huge* in some way. High drama, big stakes, messy, dirty, weird, like you're on the precipice of some huge cliff about to fall off the edge, something that will instantly pique the audience's interest and have them hanging on for the full picture. But don't forget, having a cool story is one thing, telling it in an intriguing way is another, but the most important part is how that connects to your fundamental message. In Zak Ebrahim's talk, the core of his story is how to create different outcomes, how he walked a different path to his father, the person in the opening story who killed another man. As always, everything should be in service of your message.

It might surprise you to learn that one of the areas where this approach can be effective is research. There's a belief that you have to present research findings in a linear way, but I've found that if you start with the findings and reverse back to show the process that got you there before concluding with a 'what's next', that can really help to keep people engaged from the start.

Sparklines

Time to get meta and talk about a TED talk about public speaking!

Back in 2011, Nancy Duarte gave a TED talk that kind of invented a whole new story structure. She was – and still is – an expert in presentation and communication skills, and she had something really special to share. In her talk 'The secret structure of great talks', she contrasts the instinctive brilliance of stories with the dry, uninspiring idea of presentation, and tries to figure out how to incorporate storytelling into presentations.

She takes two examples of famously excellent speeches that are routinely held up as the gold standard of compelling communication: Martin Luther King Jr's 'I Have a Dream' speech, and Steve Jobs' 2007 iPhone launch presentation.

In Nancy Duarte's approach, just like in The Hero's Journey or the Pixar Pitch, you have to begin with the ordinary world, or as Nancy calls it, 'the world as is'. The key is that she then asks you to contrast that with what could be, and emphasises that the gap between the current status quo, or 'the world as is', and the world that could be (which is where your idea has come to fruition), needs to be as big as possible. The current status quo is commonplace, while your idea is extraordinary, and the gulf between them is vast. In thinking about the openings of talks or stories in the previous section, where we mentioned Amplification, and that pops up again here. It's important to amplify the ordinariness of the status quo *as well* as how great or different life would be if your idea became a reality.

The structure within Sparklines is a bouncing ball between what is and what could be, going back and forth to emphasise how undesirable the status quo actually is when contrasted with the beautiful possibilities of your core message, which we keep being reminded of.

After this back-and-forth bouncing ball, you finish with a Call To Action, which hopefully, by this point in your talk or presentation, will be so irresistible to the audience because you've done such an incredible job of contrasting the dreary world as it is and the utopian vision of a world where your idea has been enacted.

Now, it's not to say that in order to give a good talk or presentation you *must* follow this approach, but it's interesting to see the way Nancy visually overlays her structure onto both the Martin Luther King Jr and Steve Jobs speeches, and how it does definitely map onto both of them. It's an elegant way of getting to the heart of the issue and asking your audience to psychologically and emotionally invest in a different, hopefully better, world based around your core message.

As an aside, it's also just a really nice TED talk to watch to get you all fired up and impassioned about the power of storytelling! Nancy talks with such love for stories and spreading ideas that hopefully you'll come away feeling excited to share yours too.

Nested Loops

Okay, buckle up: of all the storytelling structures, Nested Loops is probably the most complex (and not just because the name comes from computer programming!). This is one of the reasons why I said, back at the beginning of this section, that I only recommend this for longer-form content – you kind of *need* a lot of content for this structure to make sense.

The main concept here is the idea of layering narratives within each other. At the centre is your most important story, the one that most effectively shares your core message. Then, around it, you begin other stories that contribute to the audience's understanding of that central story, or add depth or context that it otherwise might lack, other perspectives, different ways of thinking about it.

The main reason to use the Nested Loops structure is where you have stories that overlap each other in some way, but without necessarily being chronological or with another kind of 'logical' way of structuring them. It's a method of arranging things that allows you to start stories in one place and end them in a different part of the talk, linking them together so they end up not *feeling* like discrete stories, and instead they're interwoven to form part of a whole.

If you want to watch a talk that might help get your head around Nested Loops, I recommend Chimamanda Ngozi Adichie's 'The danger of a single story', which, appropriately enough, is about the weight, the complexity and the power of storytelling. One of the reasons this talk works so well is that Chimamanda Ngozi Adichie is an utterly assured storyteller, a master of her craft. I would say, in general, that writers often find the more complex storytelling approaches more manageable and less daunting.

Structures to consider when more than one person is presenting

Obviously you can still use any of the structures mentioned earlier in this book if you're in a group scenario, but there are two structures that I think work better when there's more than one speaker.

Petal structure

Imagine you're drawing a flower. Not a wild, exotic flower, just a regular daisy. A cartoon flower, if you will. How would you do that? First you'd draw a circle in the middle – the yellow part of the daisy – and then you'd draw the white petals coming off it, right? That's how we want to think of this storytelling approach.

It's about that movement of your pencil from the centre, then out, and then back into the centre again. The petals all stem from that one central circle.

This structure works really well when you have a set of stories or examples or data points that all revolve around one central idea. It's a way of presenting the audience with an array of things (anecdotes, data, case study) that may, on the face of it, seem disparate, but you are showing them that they are interconnected by a central theme. The structure goes core message – evidence – core message – evidence – core message – evidence, where the 'evidence' is different every time but the core message remains the same.

The Petal approach is about coming back to the core idea multiple times throughout the talk or presentation, and that's how it differs from the 'point-story-point' structure, where you present the point at the beginning and the end with a story in the middle. It's the repeated nature of going out and coming back in, combined with the fact you're trying to bring together many different 'things' (whether that's stories, anecdotes, research) while repeating the core idea. Because of this multiplicity, it can also be a nice one to use when more than one person is speaking as part of the same presentation.

If you're finding it hard to imagine what the Petal structure looks like in practice, I would recommend watching Roman Krznaric's TED talk, 'Lessons from history for a better future'. Roman looks at the present moment – what he refers to as a 'polycrisis' – and takes lessons from everywhere from Edo-era Japan to ninth-century Cordoba to the writings of Goethe to see how we can shape our future. It's elegant and it works.

Converging Ideas

Converging Ideas takes a different approach to the Petal structure, where you're always starting and coming back to the same place. Instead, with Converging Ideas, it's like different rivers that all come together to reach the same sea. The 'rivers' may have started in different places but, by the end, they are all part of the same thing. Each story is distinct. The craft of this storytelling approach is making the ways in which they converge to become the same thing feel really clear to the audience. The book *Caste: The Origins of Our Discontents* (2020) by Isabel Wilkerson, and Ava DuVernay's 2023 movie based on it, *Origin*, come to mind when I think of this structure. In it, Wilkerson explores the social hierarchies in America, India and Nazi Germany, and draws the conclusion that these hierarchies cannot be attributed to one race or religion or economic class, but instead to the idea of caste.

Deciding on the right approach

When trying to decide which structure is the best fit for your story and your message, think about how much content you have, consider whether it's formal or informal, and how many people are speaking. Hopefully, when you think about the story you're trying to tell in your presentation or talk or conversation, it gives you some clues about the right structure to help share that story most effectively. And don't overlook the simple fact of what you *like* the most. To borrow an expression from Marie Kondo, what sparks joy for you?

How to use analogy and metaphor

Often, you're asked to speak in public because you're viewed as an expert in a particular field or have experience that might be useful to share. That means you are speaking from a position where you have knowledge or context that the audience doesn't. You might need to communicate technical concepts or new research that the audience is unfamiliar with, interpret data, or explain a new innovation. It can be exciting, but maybe a little daunting too. Speakers often have a mental barrier around how to translate their more high-level ideas into a format that's digestible for the audience, which I always think is one of the most valuable pieces of the public speaking puzzle to consider. We *want* the audience to leave feeling enthused and informed, so it's important that we communicate those ideas in language that they understand. Enter . . . analogies and metaphors.

If it wasn't obvious by now, let me tell you: I love an analogy. I love a metaphor. I love a little story to help explain my point. In general, I think these things can be extremely useful and illuminating when it comes to public speaking and storytelling. The question is, as ever, how do you use these tools to make your public speaking better?

The biggest key to making analogies or metaphors work for you and your audience is to exclusively and intentionally use language that already exists in your audience's world. Use ideas, concepts and references they have access to in their lives that will help level the playing field, or push through people's mental blocks to understanding your complex ideas. The purpose of an analogy is to make the idea you're communicating immediately comprehensible, so you need to be speaking in terms that you know will be understood by your audience. You don't want to create a situation where you need another analogy to explain your analogy! As always, it's vital to think about the audience. If you're using cultural references, are they likely to be understood by and relevant to your audience? Are your analogies appropriate to the tone of your talk, or are you suddenly slipping into a register that's super casual or formal and out of step with the event?

The next thing to think about is how to make things straightforward without being simplistic. We know you're using a metaphor or analogy because you're trying to communicate something the audience might not understand otherwise. That already puts you at an advantage over them, so we want to avoid anything that might make them feel patronised or talked down to. Again, it's all about finding the right tone, the right register, the right set of references that explain your ideas as truthfully as possible in the appropriate way for the audience, who you see as intelligent enough to understand the ideas along with you, if given the right way of thinking about them.

Another vital consideration is that while we're trying to use more generalist language, or find images that are easier to comprehend, we don't want to start dealing in clichés or hackneyed phrases. I remember, once upon a time, when I was doing pitch coaching for startups – the first time I heard someone describe their business as being 'the Uber for [insert product here]' or 'the Airbnb for [insert industry here]', I thought 'Oh, what a smart way of putting it! Now I understand what they do!', because I'd never heard it expressed like that before. Obviously, within about six months, I was hearing it *all* the time. What once felt illuminating had quickly stepped into the realm of a joke. It wasn't that what they were saying had become less true – yes, their business model *was* like Uber for x or Airbnb for y – it was that this turn of phrase had been overused by startups so intensely that our ears stopped really hearing it. This is the *exact* opposite effect to the one you want your analogy to have! You're trying to get the audience to really hear you by making your complex ideas more digestible, not making them feel so throwaway that your turn of phrase slips past their ears without their brain even noticing.

The magic with using metaphors and analogies is trying to find the sweet spot between making something feel more accessible to your audience without undermining their belief that you know, on a deep and fundamental level, what you're talking about. We want the audience to perceive you as the expert in your field, but one who's capable of translating the more complex ideas into images or stories that they can hold onto. It'll also make them more likely to remember the key ideas and more able to share them with others, which is surely what this is all about.

> If you want a phenomenal example of a talk that uses analogies and metaphors to communicate complex ideas clearly to a generalist audience, may I recommend Kathryn A. Whitehead's 'The tiny balls of fat that could revolutionize medicine', a TED talk about mRNA vaccinations and how they work. This should feel like a completely overwhelming topic to most people without a background in biochemical engineering or medicine. She explains, however, that mRNA is like a glass vase you want to send someone through the post, but you're not using a box or bubble wrap, and you're not writing their address on the package. This image immediately shows us that Professor Whitehead wants the audience to understand two key things about mRNA in its natural state: one, that it is incredibly fragile, and two, that it needs to be told where to go within the body. Creating this analogy gives the audience the foundation to understand everything else she wishes to communicate about the lipid nanoparticle technology that has changed the game

for mRNA vaccines because they form the perfect packing materials for the mRNA 'glass vase'. She uses language and images that already exist in the audience's world, takes an approach that is simple but not simplistic, and none of what she's saying feels clichéd. A great example of how to use analogy! And there are two more analogies she uses in the same talk. If you go and watch it, try to pick up on what they are.

How to wrap things up

The end is near, and so you face the final curtain... The moment that all of your beautifully-planned talk has been leading up to, the point where all the members of your audience are going to want to leap out of their seats and run from the room because they feel so energised by your message! The only problem is, you don't *quite* know how to finish it. Fear not! There are a few tried and tested storytelling-focused approaches to bringing your talk or presentation to a close. Ending on a high will dramatically increase your chances of sparking change and having your ideas listened to, and it's all about finding the perfect match between the message and the medium to get your audience to come along with you after the talk has ended. Some of the storytelling structures I shared with you earlier actually have endings built in, which could make your life feel a bit easier, or could instead make you feel limited. It's okay to take what you need from different elements and compose something that's uniquely yours.

Now you've done the hard work of bringing the audience on this beautiful journey with you, we don't want to just leave them hanging. Here are a few ways to wrap things up.

Call To Action

If you're not familiar with a Call To Action (or CTA), go into your email inbox and open an email from a brand that's trying to sell you something. Odds are, you'll see the words 'SHOP NOW' somewhere in the email. Or if not that, maybe 'use code' or the more subtle 'discover more'. Their goal is to get you to click a link on the email so you end up on their website, with the ultimate goal of returning to the original call to action: SHOP NOW. The brand is telling you what it wants you to do.

This is essentially the same with public speaking: you are telling the audience what you want them to do now they've listened to your speech and heard your core message.

People like a CTA and I do understand why: it's active. The clue's in the title. There's an *action* involved. You're able to be clear and explicit about what you want people to do.

Unfortunately, I feel as if the dominant wisdom right now is that every talk or presentation *must* end with a CTA, and that this is the only possible and logical way to end. I would disagree: you are not a marketing email from your favourite clothing brand. I think the Call To Action must be an intentionally chosen way to end your talk that fits the purpose of what you're trying to communicate. If you have a Call To Action – if you *truly* have one – then use it. But don't make one up because you think you need it for your ending. I promise there are other ways to end! Sometimes your Call To Action can be explicit: I work a lot in philanthropy, so obviously the Call To Action is 'please give us money', but you don't necessarily want to make it that explicit, so it's also about finding all the other elements as well as that CTA that will help you wrap up your presentation.

This is not to say that it's always wrong to end with a CTA. But if you use one, you have to have earned the right to ask your audience to do something. You have to have motivated or energised them enough with your talk that the Call To Action really lands. If you know you want to end with a Call To Action, that fact should have determined how you structured the content right up until that point, and the content should be compelling and well crafted enough that the audience will feel as if you've earned the right to make that demand. A speaker that comes to mind is Payzee Mahmod, who campaigns to end child marriage and honour-based abuse. I've worked with Payzee and I know how deeply affecting her talks are, how much effort and precision she puts into them, and that every time she speaks it's in service of a goal of ending child marriage. For Payzee, the Call To Action is *the point*. 'I always ask myself, what is the most relevant thing I can tell these people to do?' she told me. 'The Call To Action has to always be there. No matter who I'm speaking to, literally, the Call To Action very often is: I want you to watch my TEDx talk, and after you've watched it, I want you to share it with somebody. Or, you know, Scotland is still waiting to change their legal age of marriage, I'm thinking about working on that right now, so can you follow my social media and you'll see the actions I'm going to post for you to follow. I always have a Call To Action.'

So while a Call To Action can be a powerful tool, make sure you've both figured out the *specific* thing you want your audience to do, and make sure you've done the groundwork to convince them that it's worth doing. I would recommend going to watch Payzee's talk, 'A survivor's plea to end child marriage', to see just how this can be done.

Take A Stand (with me)

Sometimes, especially when you *feel* as if you want to end with a Call To Action but don't quite have that specific thing you want to ask your audience to do, the answer is the Take A Stand closing.

This ending is about making a personal commitment to what you're going to do. It's very powerful when you hear a speaker tell you how *they're* going to address an issue, the practical things that they're going to do to make the difference, the changes they might make in their life or the kind of work they're going to be doing now they have the knowledge and experience that has changed them. What this does is inspire the audience to want to join the speaker and to take that stand with them. It can feel like a Call To Action, but instead of telling the audience what they should do, you're telling them what *you're* going to do and inviting them to join you. The invitation part is important. It's not a demand for change but an invitation to change, an invitation to come along with you. Importantly, your commitments should be specific and not clichéd. It's not about saying 'I believe there will be a better world'. It's about narrowing it down to the kinds of changes you want to see in order to achieve that better world and committing to how you're going to play a part in that. The audience wants to know what they're signing up for!

In many cases, I find Take A Stand is a superior alternative to CTA. It feels more expansive, a way of bringing the audience in and getting them invested in your fight. People much prefer to feel as if they're being invited in to do something alongside others, rather than feeling as if they're being told to do something on their own.

I'd recommend watching Rachel Botsman's excellent talk 'We've stopped trusting institutions and started trusting strangers' for an example of how to get this really right. She closes the talk with the words: 'For my part, I want to help people understand this new era of trust so that we can get it right and we can embrace the opportunities to redesign systems that are more transparent, inclusive and accountable.' She situates herself within the dynamic she's just laid out, and states that she wants to be part of the solution. It's a powerful invitation to join her.

Zoom Out

This is one of my favourite ways to end a talk. The Zoom Out is pretty self-explanatory: think of a camera lens that for a long time has been trained on a small corner of the action in a scene, and then zooms out to give you a bigger perspective on the same scene. One of the things that can make a compelling talk, or even just a compelling conversation, is specificity. Showing that you have specific ideas or using specific examples rather than speaking in generalities can be extremely powerful, but it can also be beneficial to show the bigger picture along with these more close-up moments. A structure where you're bouncing back and forth between the small-scale and the large-scale can feel confusing to the listener, so the Zoom Out allows you to stay focused for the main part of your talk or presentation or conversation *and then*, at the end, give the wider scale, the bigger picture, locating your idea within geography, within time, within a body of research. The power – as it so often does – comes from the contrast, from the variation in scale. Playing with proportions is a well-used tactic in high fashion, and I would recommend applying it here too.

The Zoom Out can be a great approach if you've been dealing in issues that feel really practical, or even small. With the

Zoom Out, you can show how even these small changes you're proposing, this seemingly mundane idea that you're fixated on trying to share, is part of a much bigger picture and is contributing to a whole that the audience hasn't been able to see yet.

Donnel Baird, founder of climate tech company BlocPower, used a Zoom Out to close his talk 'Why you should ditch deadly fossil fuel appliances': 'If we can electrify one building, it means that we can electrify a whole block of buildings. If we can electrify a block of buildings, it means that we can electrify a neighbourhood. If we can electrify a neighbourhood, it means that we can electrify a city. And if we can electrify a city, that means we can electrify a country.' Yours doesn't have to be quite so literal, but it shows you the idea in practice!

Callback

Quite simply, a Callback ending is about referencing things from your talk and using them again to close. If you think about pulling those threads that were running through your talk, it's a way of bringing them together to help you end. It could be a really light reference to something you said earlier or it could be something much more serious. An example of a Callback can be found in Sofie Hagen's talk, 'You can be fat and happy'. It begins with an anecdote about when they were eating a burger in public and realised they were being filmed and mocked by strangers at another table. They then return to this story at the end – hence the Callback – in a way that allows them to wrap up the talk with a powerful message. The important thing is that even *without* the Callback at the end, the opening story stood very much on its own, and the Callback just added new layers to it. The audience didn't spend Sofie's whole talk wondering what the relevance was: the relevance was obvious, and the Callback functioned as a really elegant little added bonus at the end.

I really like Galina Angarova's talk, 'The hidden cost of the green transition's mineral rush' too, to demonstrate a callback. She opens the talk with an anecdote of something a trusted elder from her indigenous community told her, and then closes by returning to the same conversation. Galina literally says, 'So when I go back to my conversation with the trusted elder . . .': it really can be as simple as that.

The Callback works especially well when the audience doesn't know the second half of the story is even coming, but just like with Sofie's talk, the first part of the story needs to work well enough on its own to not leave the audience distracted.

Reframe with a twist

This way of ending is about providing a completely different perspective or angle on the thing you've been talking about and leaving people with a bit of a question or an element of surprise. It's not about sending your talk off in a completely different direction or bringing in entirely new content at the last minute, and it's definitely not about undermining everything you've spent your talk or presentation carefully laying out for the audience. Instead it's about expanding the ways of thinking about the issue, going beyond the ideas you've laid out so far and leaving the audience with a curiosity they're hopefully going to pursue when they leave the room. It's also a way to get them to think more curiously about other issues, applying this way of thinking beyond this specific case.

If you want a great example of an ending that uses this approach, watch the economist Daniel Susskind's '3 myths about the future of work (and why they're not true)', which lays out the key issues facing the world of work now we have entered the age of artificial intelligence. By the end, despite acknowledging all of the frankly frightening challenges facing workers now, he argues we're actually in a better position than our ancestors. 'How to make sure that everyone gets a slice of the pie . . . won't be easy . . . but this is a far better problem to have than the one that haunted our ancestors for centuries: how to make that pie big enough in the first place.'

Again, when you're figuring out which ending to choose, look to the rest of your talk or presentation to guide you: your opening and your chosen structure possibly will lend themselves to specific closings. Ask yourself questions about your purpose and what you want the audience to do or what you want to leave them with, and the right ending should become more apparent to you.

Section 3
Delivery

Why delivery matters
(after you've done everything else)

You've made it! You've done all the hard and necessary work to get here. From knowing you're going to speak in some capacity to making a solid plan for what you want to share, and who you want to share it with, to making big decisions about how you're going to integrate storytelling into your talk or conversation or presentation, and the specific structures and techniques you're going to use. Now we get to really think about the actual *moment itself*. The point where you step onto the stage or stand up at the wedding or pitch to those potential new clients or sit down to have that important conversation. The bit that was probably making you the most nervous. It's time to confront it.

This is the part of cooking your delicious dinner-party meal where you think about the plating, the presentation, everything that will allow your guests to feel that they're really having an experience and that they're in the hands of a master chef. All the things that aren't *really* about the ingredients and how you've combined them but about how they look at the end of the process. Although I've said before that I think this is actually the least vital stage of the process, it's still really important, and I know it's something that people lose a lot of sleep over.

That said, I'm hopeful that now you're actually here, at this point in your journey to public speaking, you feel slightly less nervous about it. That's because – ideally – you've proved to yourself that you have a wealth of knowledge, have tailored it to your audience and your message, and that you've found the most elegant and engaging possible ways of framing it for them. This should have given you at least a little bit of confidence that you're totally competent to do this work, but, if not, you now have a whole section ahead of you later in this book about the idea of 'impostor syndrome', so maybe wait until you've read that before you freak out.

In this part of the book, however, we're going to be thinking about the way you speak, and whether it's acceptable and appropriate to use your own 'real' voice (spoiler alert: it is). We're going to be thinking about how you move, both as that relates to your body and also to the clothes you wear. If you're feeling nervous about having to learn lines like an actor, we're going to think a lot about the idea of scripting and internalisation, preparation and rehearsal. A lot of people don't need visuals for their talks, but sometimes you will, so there's a section on slide decks coming. We even explore how to approach feedback, and what kind of feedback is useful versus the kind that just gets in your head without actually helping you. And then, as mentioned, there's the looming spectre of 'impostor syndrome', something that I've *really* changed my mind about after a lot of time, thought and research.

Substance over style, always

All these things might sound like they're largely 'aesthetic', and, of course, I was loudly banging my drum in the first section about how content is more important than style. While that's true, because it forms the foundation of everything that comes after, I know that all the things we're going to think about in terms of delivery in this section are the things that will give you that greater feeling of calm and grounded confidence that will allow you to unlock your authentic self and deliver the idea that you've been wanting to share, all with an engaged audience in the palm of your hand.

The fact is, and it probably won't come as a surprise to hear me say it, being an expert in your field is not necessarily enough to be a great public speaker. Having the knowledge in your head means nothing if you can't metabolise that knowledge and communicate it to other people in a way that makes sense and resonates with you and them. That's what I hope you've learned from this book so far: all the practical skills that it takes to turn knowledge, passion and experience into a compelling and memorable talk.

Now, let's wrap things up and give you that final boost to get you over the finish line . . .

Finding your authentic voice

Back in the day, the people we considered experts worth listening to were older white men in grey suits. Then came the radical moment when we started listening to ... middle-aged white men in black turtlenecks. I hope we're finally ready to progress to the next level, where you can look like anyone and come from anywhere and be considered an expert, as well as a natural fit for public speaking. We're already living in a moment where Greta Thunberg, Alexandria Ocasio-Cortez and Munroe Bergdorf are understood to be excellent communicators. Are you ready to join them, or are you still holding your real self back?

When I mentioned the turtleneck, I was, of course, referencing Steve Jobs. Now, think of that famous iPhone presentation at MacWorld in 2007 (or look it up if you haven't seen it before). His style of communication is so specific, dare I say iconic, but what would it feel like if *everyone* spoke like him? It would be boring, because as the old saying goes, variety is the spice of life. So the key is not to copy other successful communicators, but to figure out the parts of yourself, your personality, your experience, your voice – both literal and metaphorical – that make you who you are. It's about learning how to harness those things to give your audience the most effective and memorable way of receiving your message.

You are a mixing deck not a light switch

People often ask me if they're allowed to speak like *themselves*, or if they're meant to have some kind of public speaking persona, like a posh 'telephone voice'. I'm very confident in saying that the answer is always to be yourself. But what does 'yourself' mean? How do you stay true to your authentic voice? Figuring this out can feel overwhelming, but I really encourage you not to think of authenticity as an on/off switch, that either you're being 'yourself' or you're not, and therefore you're being inauthentic. Instead I like to look at it as a mixing deck that a sound engineer might use. Think of all the different parts of yourself, all the things that make you who you are. Whether that's irreverent, funny, energetic, empathetic, whatever characteristics you possess, you know that you're not operating at 100 per cent of each of these things 100 per cent of the time. The fact that you're not peak energetic or peak irreverent when you're at a funeral doesn't mean you're not being your authentic self, it just means you're turning down those parts of you as the occasion requires, and maybe turning up the empathetic part instead.

Try to become really clear on what these elements of your personality are. When you think about your 'authentic self', what actually *are* those characteristics that you think are essential to you? That's the first step towards being able to master them, enhancing and reducing them as the situation requires. And remember: there is no such thing as a trait that is inherently good or bad in a public speaker. If you think you're too quiet, maybe what you actually are is considered. If you think you're too enthusiastic, maybe that's a really infectious passion.

I think the most important thing is reassuring yourself that you're not creating some sort of fake persona when you're public speaking, just because you're amplifying some parts of yourself over others. This is actually something we do all the time, intuitively. The characteristics you amplify when communicating with a toddler are not the same as the ones you amplify when communicating with your boss, but that doesn't mean that in both situations you're being 'fake'. The core of what you're saying always remains the same, and that's non-negotiable. Again, as with many, many parts of public speaking and storytelling, it's all about audience. How do you match up your authentic public speaking self with the needs of your audience? Once you bridge that gap, you've done a lot of the work already.

What does it mean to be professional?

Amid any talk of bringing your authentic self to public speaking, it's also vital to start unpicking the messages you might have internalised about what makes someone 'professional' or 'an expert'. Believing these messages is not your fault: there's a huge amount of gatekeeping in most professions and fields of study that can make them feel exclusionary of working-class people, people of colour, women, disabled people, people with regional accents, and many more. All of which is to say that it's not surprising that you're wondering if you have to put on the public speaking equivalent of a 'phone voice'. Wondering if you have to conceal the things that make you who you are and that might set you apart from other people in your field. I would truthfully say no. I believe that part of the key to unlocking your unique power in public speaking is bringing your own voice – literally and metaphorically – to the stage. Being *you* is what has led you to this point, the point where you have knowledge and experience and are being called upon to share that with an audience. It's also likely to have informed the way you relate to that knowledge and expertise.

My friend and *Climate Curious* podcast co-host Ben Hurst is a Black man and I wanted to get his perspective on this. He's an amazing speaker, and when you watch the audience listen to him speak, you can tell he has them transfixed. When I was chatting to him for this book, the idea of code-switching came up, and if you're not familiar with it, code-switching in a racial context is a strategy where Black people adjust the way they present themselves to reflect the norms and behaviours of the dominant group in certain situations, largely to be perceived as 'more professional'.

'Code-switching is such an interesting one, because I think it's a choice, but I think it often doesn't feel like a choice,' Ben said. 'People do it out of necessity. People do it out of habit. But it is, to me, a decision that you make, and the decision that comes with big consequences. So sometimes, if you're in a situation and you need to code switch and you don't do it, you can pay the price. Like, there's a cost to that. You can still do the job no matter who you are, as long as you know the skills and you're able to remember the information, you can do the thing. So I think all of the rest of it is just like style points in the Olympics, it's how you want to finesse it and how you want to do it. But I also think there's something quite subversive and deeply political about forcing that, from my perspective. I think it's important to not code switch, because I do believe it gives other people permission to not have to do it. And, and it's also boring, I just want to be how I am.'

Being given the right to speak like yourself, and being *actively encouraged* to speak like yourself, is hopefully also a way to give yourself permission to drop the jargon. When did you last use technical jargon in everyday conversations? Jonathan Foley, one of the world's top climate scientists and science communicators, is well aware that this is something that many people worry about, especially when talking about science. He's clear on the need to communicate *accurately*, which, for him, means more than just saying something that is true. 'An accurate message is one that's received and understood clearly. If it's never received you didn't do the damn work. So get rid of the jargon, keep it simple and stop flexing.' What if we turned the idea of authenticity to our advantage and, instead of worrying about whether we're being formal enough, used it as an opportunity to make things feel more accessible to our audience? No need to flex when you're speaking like your authentic self. Instead of jargon-flexing, the goal should be to communicate so others understand.

Master your material

I would argue – and I know other speakers would agree with me – that part of having the confidence to speak like yourself and use your own authentic voice is having a deep familiarity and mastery of your material. It can be liberating, in fact, and climate communicator Rebecca Fisher agrees. 'I think a huge part of it is being really confident in what you're saying. Knowing I've looked at this from all angles, this is what I do day in and day out, I'm confident in it, has allowed me to be much more authentic,' she told me.

When we talk about 'speaking like you', we mean speaking like the *real* you, and not some public speaking version of you. Speakers often worry about being perceived as inauthentic, and I find that being your authentic self and speaking in your authentic voice means trying to figure out who you are when you're not performing. Briar Goldberg, TED's Director of Speaker Coaching, told me: 'The minute you act like you're acting, or that you're performing, and you don't sound like the same person that people would see at the cocktail hour after the event, they're getting two different versions of you. And that's weird: we don't talk to each other like that. So the minute you turn into this performative version of yourself, that's when you get the feedback that you're inauthentic, and I think it can feel really biting.'

Treat everyday life as a practice run for public speaking. What are the personality traits or behaviours you're using when you have interactions in everyday situations that make you feel good? Think about the feedback you get from the people around you, at work or in your circle of friends, and how can you lean into the great parts of yourself to make your public speaking even more authentically you, rather than less.

It can feel a bit overwhelming to try to access your authentic voice, especially when you've spent time and energy trying to suppress it. There are a few questions you can ask yourself that might help.

- Why are you the best person to speak about this – what do you bring to it that is unique to you?
- What feeling do you want the audience to have while listening to you?
- How can you bring your personality to your talk?
- How can you construct your talk so that you connect with your audience as if you're having a conversation with one person?

Maryam Pasha

The best way for you to communicate with your audience is to try to stay as true as you can to your authentic self while also serving that particular audience's needs. For example, ironing out your accent probably won't serve their needs, but it might be useful to make sure you add context to anecdotes that have a particular relevance to your culture but not theirs. But if your question is: are you allowed to be doing this work? Nobody can tell your story better than you can, I promise.

What to do with your hands (and other things)

Knowing you have great content is one thing, but have you thought about what it'll be like to actually deliver it? What your body will feel like, how you'll move around the meeting room or the stage, what that space will even look like, what you'll be wearing? If not, definitely start thinking (and asking questions!) now.

As actor turned speaker coach Sivan Sasson told me: 'public speaking is a full-body experience'. Obviously, focusing on the content is really important, but don't forget about the *experience* of delivering that content.

Make it intentional

Body language is something that seems to loom large in new speakers' minds, and it's easy to come across a lot of advice in this area. The problem is, that advice is often contradictory! So instead of getting too bogged down in the science of body language and trying to figure out the exact 'right' way to gesture or move around the stage, I'm just going to say that there is no one single magic answer. Instead, we want to find the perfect expression of you and your knowledge and your experience and your content that is *intentional* but is not *rehearsed*.

What I mean by that is if you watched a video of yourself speaking, are there any little nervous or inadvertent ways you move or gesture that would surprise you, and make you go 'Oh! I didn't know I did that!'? I'm talking about things like touching your hair, twisting your wedding ring, pacing around, playing with your earrings. These are probably not *intentional* movements, they're just habits that don't serve a useful purpose to you as a speaker. It's a fine line: you're not acting, and I'm not asking you to rehearse your hand movements or the way you walk around the stage, but I do want you to think about how to make your movements intentional rather than accidental. Trying to find that intentionality can also feel empowering. Instead of letting yourself perform these unintentional movements or habits, you are making a decision to do them as part of your talk or presentation. 'When you call it a decision, I think it makes you more powerful,' says Sivan Sasson. 'It makes you feel like the boss of whatever is happening. It's not just happening. No, you decided to do this, it makes you more responsible for everything.'

Jennifer Kitt is President of Climate Lead and works to increase philanthropic funding for climate projects. She has a lot of experience in speaking to philanthropists, corporations and foundations, and has seen first hand how easy it is to let these unintentional habits creep in. She told me about a time in her previous job at Stanford University, where she was

Chief Development Officer for their Medical Centre. 'When I was at Stanford, they did a video of all of us, and I would always tilt my head when I would speak to an audience,' she said. 'And the feedback I got was, *You're giving away all your power when you do that; you have just made yourself into a little girl*. It was super cringey to see me trying to make myself into someone approachable. I can tell I still do that in conversations, but I'm able to notice and fix it.'

It's easy to get overwhelmed with all the various wisdoms of psychology and body language that says things like 'having your hands on your hips makes you look bossy' or 'holding your hands behind your back means you're hiding something'. Instead of fixating on those small ideas in isolation, think of your movements and gestures as part of a whole: someone who's got great content who's well prepared is less likely to be undermined by one body language 'trait' than someone who's under-prepared and doesn't know what they're going to say.

Making eye contact

Although I said at the beginning of the book that this wasn't about teaching you *one weird trick*, there are occasionally little tricks and tips that I come across that feel genuinely useful. I picked up this interesting tip from the comedian Sofie Hagen, which they called 'the W'. 'If you don't want to look directly at people in the audience, you want to make a W with your gaze: look up, down, middle, down, up, and just casually let your eye move. Not super quick, but if you find a natural pace, then people feel more involved.'

Don't erase yourself

Unfortunately, this is made a lot harder when you're someone that might be stereotyped by the audience. We know that, for example, middle-aged white men can 'get away' with a lot more than, for example, young Black women, which has way more to do with our culture and society than it does with any dos and don'ts of public speaking. I completely understand wanting to come off as polished and professional as possible, but I would recommend doing that with your content and delivery, rather than trying to erase all signs of your own unique life and story from your speaking.

Something I often have to work on with my speakers is liberating them from the public speaking equivalent of 'polite phone voice'. For some reason, people tend to get a bit quiet, posh and embarrassed when they first start public speaking. One way I've found to get around this is getting my speakers to talk *really loudly*, sometimes even shout, just to see what it feels like. Whatever it takes to help them break out of that 'phone voice' and become not only more themselves, but literally more audible to the audience. My friend Simon Bucknall has coached a lot of people in public speaking, and I'm happy to say that he agrees: 'Speaking louder feels uncomfortable, but it energises the voice. It brings urgency. The difficulty is that when you speak more loudly than comfortable . . . it feels a bit weird! But over time, it can be strangely empowering and energising as a speaker.'

Ask lots of questions

If you're speaking in a more formal setting, ahead of the day of your talk or presentation, it's completely fine to ask the organiser questions about the set up. In fact, I would recommend trying to find out as much information as possible to help you make decisions.

Here are some examples of questions I ask:

- *Will I be on a raised platform?* If you're on a raised platform, everything you wear will appear shorter, so you might find yourself feeling self-conscious about the length of your skirt, or suddenly become aware that you are wearing socks you didn't realise anyone would be able to see.
- *What kind of microphone will I have?* If you're on a lapel mic or headset, you will need somewhere to clip the mic pack, which may be an issue if you're wearing something without pockets. If you're using a handheld microphone and also are using a clicker for your slides, then you won't have a hand to hold your notes in.
- *Am I sitting down or standing?* I like to know if I'm on a chair or a high stool. As a shorter, rounder person, I find a high stool is my personal nemesis, so I want to know about it in advance!

- *Is this being recorded?* This might impact what you say or whether you share proprietary information.
- *Who's in the audience?* Get as much insight as possible into who's there and why.

Making conscious decisions about these points means not only will you feel more relaxed and confident on the day, but also means your mind is more free to focus on the speaking part, not the moving or clothing part.

Avoid technical issues

If your speaking engagement is to a large audience, it may involve some kind of amplification, which will generally mean either a microphone on stage or you wearing a mic pack. This is something that it's really useful to know about in advance, because both will affect how you move. Have you thought about how holding a microphone might affect the way you gesture or walk around onstage? Have you ever rehearsed your talk imagining you're holding a microphone? And if you're wearing a mic pack, this will have an impact on the clothes you wear: you'll need a collar to clip the microphone onto, and then a pocket or waistband in which to store the wired pack (yet another reason to put pockets on women's clothing!). Asking these questions ahead of time will allow you to make the best choices as you prepare, and lighten your cognitive load when you need it most, not to mention reducing the stress of unexpected surprises.

Standing or sitting?

And if your speaking engagement *isn't* formal and isn't to a large audience? It can still be useful to ask what kind of space you'll be in, whether you'll be behind a table or standing or sitting on a high stool. Having this kind of information can help you choose comfortable clothing *and* means you won't feel caught off-guard on the day.

If you're going to be standing rather than sitting, have a think about *how* you're going to stand. How do you stand when you're not moving? What do you do with your arms? When I'm standing or sitting still during a calm, non-public speaking moment, what am I doing? Give yourself this place to come back to. Test out different options, and understand that what might *feel* relaxed to you might end up looking tense and awkward to the audience, and vice versa. Try to find a happy place where you're physically at ease *and* giving signals to the audience that you're both relaxed and engaged. You want to project composure even if you don't feel it.

Roman Krznaric, a social philosopher who focuses on the power of ideas to create change, has done a lot of public speaking. When I talked to him for this book, he brought up the way that using written notes can impact your movement. 'I'm just talking about me here, but I never, ever use notes. What that means is I never have to stand behind a lectern, and I'm always right there in front of the audience.

If there's a lectern, I tell them to take it off the stage, or I just won't use it. I want to connect directly with you.' The idea of removing any barriers between you and the audience is worth thinking about, not least because it'll probably help you feel more relaxed in the space. You don't want to feel as if you're hiding behind a lectern, or reading from notes. Finding that ease in the way you present will make the experience more pleasurable for you and your audience.

What to wear

Now . . . can we talk about your outfit? Anyone who knows me knows that I *love* clothes. Fashion is such an important part of my life, and choosing clothes for an event is part of the fun for me. But, as much as I would love to, I never choose an outfit based solely on how it looks. I choose outfits based on how they feel, and the brain space they'll give me when I'm speaking, and I would strongly recommend you do the same. I don't have the mental capacity to wonder if my dress is too short, or whether I can move my arms freely in those sleeves, or if the audience can tell I'm sweating because I've worn something too warm. I try to anticipate as many of those things as possible and choose clothes that let me focus on the job at hand, and a lot of that is tied to physical movement. Again, it's all about the cognitive load. What are the decisions you can make ahead of your event that will allow you to glide through it with the most confidence?

But decisions around clothing are also tied to how we're perceived as people. Rebecca Fisher, from the global campaign to electrify road transportation, told me: 'I've made adjustments in how I show up, because I look young and I'm a woman. I always make sure that, if anything, I'm overdressed professionally. I know personally I'm at my best when I feel confident in how I show up and how I'm dressed.'

I've said it before and I'll say it again: the 'confidence' that Rebecca references comes from knowledge and preparation. The same goes for the clothes you choose. Just like a marathon runner would *never* wear new trainers or an untested sports bra on race day, I would recommend doing the same for speaking events. Don't wear something you've never worn before, and instead stick to an outfit you know makes you feel physically comfortable. I apply the same logic to hair and makeup: don't burn your forehead trying out a cool new style with your GHDs on the morning of your job interview or TED talk! And that new mascara might have great reviews, but you don't want to put yourself at risk of itchy, irritated eyes. Speaking is hard enough, and you don't want to add extra levels of complexity or bring in new things you have to think about when your brain needs to focus on speaking.

I know it's boring, but comfortable shoes are a must. Sure, I'd look amazing in those new brogues, but do I need to break them in first? Or will I be spending the whole time worrying about a blister? Outfit selection is all about finding that perfect midpoint between things that make you look amazing but also feel comfortable. Of course, some lucky people are able to feel amazing *and* comfortable while wearing six-inch heels. One of them is my friend, the climate activist Pattie Gonia, who – if you couldn't tell from the name – also happens to be a drag queen. Now, I'm not suggesting you do your talk in drag necessarily, but I love hearing what Pattie has to say about presentation and how it interacts with the audience's expectations of you as a speaker. She talks about it as being like a Trojan Horse approach: 'I think that what I love in drag is people completely thinking that it's going to be one thing: you know, me stepping on the TED stage in an all pink outfit and being very Barbie doll, and then hitting people with things that are really, actually relatable and commonalities that we might share.' She's able to blend the more eye-catching outfits with impactful climate activism because she's deeply knowledgeable and a great communicator. It's high-level work, but it just goes to show that it can be done!

All the decisions you make about how you physically present yourself when you speak should be as intentional as possible. The more information and knowledge you have around what the space looks like and what technology requires of you should help you to make good choices and leave you to focus on the most important thing: your content.

How (not) to memorise your talk

Scripting is something I get asked about *a lot* and I wish there was a one-size-fits-all answer to this, but there isn't. It's very personal. For some people, it's useful to try to know every word they want to say, and for others that approach just won't work and they're better off using a more basic outline. But whichever approach you choose, the one thing you're *not* going to be able to avoid? Practice. You're going to be doing a lot of practising either way.

Many people think that scripting their talk will inherently take longer than using an outline, but, in my experience, it doesn't always work like that. If you use a script, you know that you have every word written down, you know it fits the time you have, and you can start internalising it. Whereas if you have an outline, you actually need just as much time because the preparation is different: you don't have every word written down, so you *then* need to prepare and practise all the different versions that might come out of your mouth when you use that outline. In the end, as with many things, the answer lies somewhere in the grey area, and most people use a hybrid of both approaches.

Someone I really wanted to talk to for this section of the book was Briar Goldberg, who is TED's Director of Speaker

Coaching, because she has so much knowledge and experience around scripting, memorisation and rehearsing. 'I'm of two minds on script writing,' she told me. 'I think it's probably the most effective way to truly sharpen your ideas to the sharpest point. I really think that if you are a person who is a communicator, and you've never actually tried to write out an argument, it's well worth it. It's the sharpest way to get to the argument, the most persuasive version of the story, and it's also the best way to make sure you're falling within the time limit you've been given, which is absolutely essential. But then you have to be willing to let it go.'

The idea of being willing to let it go is crucial. When we say 'script', obviously the first thing that comes to mind is a play: the words get written and then they become not just the definitive version but the *only* version. Actors memorise this one single document and any deviations from it are wrong. That's not how I want you to think about scripting when it comes to public speaking. You are not an actor, and I don't want you focusing your mental energy on reciting the next line, I want your mental energy to stay in the room, with your audience.

There are lots of ways to make scripting feel useful and relevant to you, and this is true for both experienced and less experienced speakers. If you're new to speaking, or if you're *not* new but you're talking about a new idea or subject, scripting is important because it's a way of sorting out your thoughts, your ideas, your stories, it allows you to make sure it all makes sense and that you haven't forgotten something crucial. Experienced speakers need scripting because they often have way too much they want to say, and scripting helps them trim, edit and refine their ideas so that you don't get to a point where your time is up and you haven't actually convinced the audience of what you're here to convince them of.

We often have mental scripts for things without even realising it: think of a story you've told over and over again, something weird or funny that happened to you. When you tell that story now, you've kind of got a mental script for it, right? You've figured out what the main 'beats' of the story are, you haven't missed the funny part, you've made sure it's not got loads of extra information that'll distract your listener. You've got a sense of the flow of what you're trying to say. That's what we're trying to achieve here: giving you the confidence that you know how your words and ideas will flow from one thing to the next, that you won't forget the important points, and that you'll be able to do it within the allotted time.

> The downside of having a script is the danger of it feeling over-rehearsed or recited. This means it can be useful to give it a more natural or conversational tone so it has a little bit more life. I've found there are a few ways to make a script feel more conversational:

- Break the rules: end sentences with prepositions, speak using sentence fragments rather than always whole sentences.
- Use informal language that is true to you and your experience.
- Use contractions (I've instead of I have) except for emphasis.
- Remove most qualifiers (this means expressions like 'a bit', 'kind of', 'maybe', 'to a degree' etc).
- Use the active voice and first person instead of passive voice in the third person ('I think' rather than 'it is often thought that . . .').
- Use the words 'you', 'I' and 'we' to draw the audience in with you.

Memorisation vs Internalisation

Once you've got your script or your outline that you're going to work from, now you have to memorise it 100 per cent, right? Wrong! One of the biggest things that I've learned from Briar is the idea of internalisation, instead of memorisation. It's not about having every single word in the exact same order every time. It's about making sure you have complete command of the flow of your content. You can convey the meaning, but the order of the specific words is not important.

And more than anything, it's about giving you the confidence and flexibility to work around the unexpected. You want to feel that you're holding on to your talk or presentation with a loose grip, rather than white-knuckling it, so if someone asks a question or there's a fire alarm or someone has a coughing fit, you can just mentally jump right back in, instead of getting derailed.

Briar is completely anti-memorisation. But that *doesn't* mean she's anti-preparation. 'You have to practise, but it should come out a little bit differently every time, because that's also how we communicate with each other. The heart of the message stays the same, even the heart of each *sentence* stays the same, but you give yourself a little flexibility to let it fall out of your mouth differently every time. So it's structured, you're meeting your time limits, you're meeting your persuasion moments, but you give yourself, you allow yourself to say it a little bit differently every time.'

If you think about what she says there, essentially there are a few non-negotiable parts that you have to be absolutely on top of: the structure, the time limits and what she calls your 'persuasion moments'. Outside of that, the actual words you're using are free to change as you see fit or based on what comes to mind in the moment.

How to do it

For some people, the approach that works to internalise your content is to start with *all* the information that you want to say and then systematically reduce and reduce the number of words you need to look at in order to be able to deliver your talk. So it may start out with needing to read every word from your script, but then you move from there to a couple of sentences per paragraph, but those are enough to get you to say the same content you were saying before. And from there, maybe down to one sentence per paragraph, then one word per paragraph, so once you can visualise each word, the whole talk comes back to you in the right order, without you needing to be reading from a script. Other people I've worked with prefer to make an audio recording of the entire talk, and then just listen to it until it becomes completely familiar to them – like lyrics to that one song from the '90s that for some reason you've never forgotten when you can't even remember the password to your email.

Now for rehearsing. Practising. Preparation. Whatever you want to call it. That's the non-negotiable part of the process. There is simply no way around it.

Every speaker I interviewed for this book, without fail, mentioned the importance of practice and preparation. When I asked my *Climate Curious* podcast co-host Ben Hurst how he gets to a place of feeling confident in his speaking, he said: 'Part of it is the hours that you get in, the amount of time that you practise doing it right, and there's no way around it. You just gotta practise it. I think part of it is really having a deep belief in what you're sharing and knowing that you know what you're talking about and what you're talking about matters.' That's something that can't be faked.

Briar – who's such a fount of knowledge that she should write her own book, which I would immediately pre-order – was absolutely firm on the necessity of practice, based on her extensive experience of coaching TED speakers: 'Nothing scares me more than speakers that say *I never practise*. I think I can say this with 100 per cent confidence: the minute somebody says that to me, I know they will not perform well.'

Please understand: you are not the exception. You are not going to be the one special person who does not need to practise, who can just wing it and wow the audience with your innate brilliance or your deep knowledge of your subject area. I've said it before and I'll say it again now, that being an expert in a particular field does not always translate to public speaking, and people that are naturally confident at speaking in public are not always necessarily good at communicating information. You've got to put the time into honing your content *and* practising delivering it if you want your moment in the spotlight to go off without a hitch. I often meet people who tell me they don't practise ahead of public speaking, and then when I see them speak I think, *well . . . yes, I can tell!* It's limiting the impact their ideas can have, and clearly no one has told them this.

I sometimes get asked how to prepare for more informal speaking opportunities, or things like job interviews, where it's not a question of internalising a large amount of content. My advice would still be to practise. That, to me, means practising the bits you *know* will happen, like introducing yourself with confidence, in a natural, calm way. Could you perhaps practise that at a party or a company away day?

I have a whole section coming up on how to get useful feedback, so I won't go into it too much here, but although most of your preparation time will probably be spent alone, it might also be useful to do a run-through in front of someone, and use the feedback questions in the upcoming section.

Practice makes perfect

Now, you've practised and you've practised and you've practised. But how do you know when you've practised *enough*? For formal situations, I would argue that you know you've got enough rehearsal time under your belt when you're not really thinking about what comes next. Better than that, when it feels as if you've moved from speaking at the audience to speaking with them, when it feels as if you're having a conversation rather than giving a speech. For something more informal, it's when you have a real sense of comfort with your content. A feeling of calm and intimacy that can't be derailed by a random question. So if you're giving a presentation at work, you know the flow of your slides and have a sense of what you're going to say about each of them and how you'll wrap everything up with confidence, even if you haven't rehearsed every single word.

And I cannot stress enough: time is of the essence! Time seems to work differently when you're on stage to anywhere else in the world, or as Briar puts it, 'there is a public speaking space-time continuum that feels different than real-life time'. This is why it's so vital to make sure that, amid all the different ways you can express your key ideas in the structure you've set out, they roughly take the same amount of time to get from your brain to your mouth.

'Off the cuff' is an illusion

Do you remember those people at school or university that seemed to do absolutely no work all term and then ace their exams? Those are the people who make you think that speaking 'off the cuff' is a good idea. You look at them onstage and they seem so casual, so unrehearsed, and you love being in their company. They're not dry, they're lively and relaxed, and you want to be a speaker just like them. But let me tell you: it's a trap. If someone is a great communicator *and* seems like they're speaking in a completely unrehearsed, offhand way, I can guarantee you that they've said what they're saying to you a thousand times before. It's not that they're speaking off the cuff, it's that they're so comfortable with their content and their structure and how to hit their key points within the time limit, and where all their stories fit within their talk, that they could deliver it in their sleep. And that's because they've *practised*.

When we think about public speaking, we think politician not comedian (and huge credit has to go to Simon Bucknall for illuminating this distinction for me!). The reason we think that is because we think that public speaking is wooden, dry, uncompelling – choose your adjective. We don't realise that comedians are actually doing public speaking too, because you feel as if they're just telling stories and talking to you as a person, 'off the cuff', when actually *that is public speaking.*

Now, since we're talking about comedians, I thought the professional comedian Sofie Hagen would be an interesting person to ask about the idea of speaking 'off the cuff'. 'I wasn't decent on stage, to the point where I could fool people into thinking I was talking "off the cuff" until I was five years in,' they told me. 'And for those five years, I had gigged between 200 and 300 times a year. So that's at least 1,000 times. Let's say each spot was an average of 10 minutes. So, 10,000 minutes on stage before it looked fairly natural, whether or not it was good. I had tested that show in particular eighty times before I did it in Edinburgh that year, before its premiere. That's eighty hours of doing the same show, the same material, the same stories.'

I'm not suggesting you need to do 10,000 minutes of practice. I suppose the thing I'm trying to say here is that the actual work of public speaking does not just happen on stage. That's maybe 20 per cent of the labour involved in public speaking, and the rest is in the preparation. My husband is, among many other things, a quiz guy. When he and his teammates made it through the auditions for a BBC quiz a few years ago, I have to confess I was taken aback to find out he was revising ahead of his first appearance. I thought you just showed up and hoped for the best. I thought wrong. And then it hit me: this is just like public speaking. Sure, you can't predict every single question you'll be asked, but, within reason, there are things you know *might* come up, and that you can actually learn, whether that's US state capitals, Shakespeare plays, the periodic table or the popes in chronological order. The preparation you do as a public speaker is your way of increasing the things you can control and decreasing the things you can't control.

But what if you get to the point where you feel like you've rehearsed too much and it's become flat? Sivan Sasson, who's both a speaker coach and an actor, has one simple tip: change something. 'Just make a change, it doesn't even matter what, because the minute something's changed, you wake up. Think of yourself at a concert. In a classical concert, I will fall asleep, and then suddenly there's a change in the music, and I wake up. So sometimes you just need to change something out of the automatic way that you've been saying it for two months.'

Fingers crossed I've sold you on the powers of internalisation versus memorisation and left you in no doubt that practising is an integral part of the process. If I leave you with nothing else, please let it be that!

Avoiding death (or boredom) by PowerPoint

When you heard you had to give a talk or a presentation, I bet the first thing you thought was *right, I've got to make slides*. Visuals are actually one of my favourite parts of public speaking to discuss, so strap in.

You might have noticed that I don't go in for absolutism. Whenever there's a technique or a principle that I'm personally not fond of, I'll still give you a decent account of it and let you decide whether your situation might be one of the rare examples where it could work. So please allow me one hard limit, which is that you should never, ever read your slides.

I know 'think about your audience' is an idea you've heard more than enough of by now, but I want you to really put yourself in your audience's shoes. Think of a presentation or a talk you've been to where someone opened up a slide deck and you just saw a wall of text, *and then the presenter started reading it*. Did your heart fill with joy and pleasure or did you get a sinking feeling? To me, watching someone read text off a slide deck is like watching someone else operate a computer: slow and frustrating. The audience can read faster than you can speak, so you really are holding them back by reading your slides aloud. If you are producing slides with a solid wall of text and then reading them aloud, what value are you actually bringing by being in the room?

Whether we're talking about PowerPoint, Google Slides, Keynote, whatever, slides are not for you. They are for your audience.

Complement don't copy

My number-one rule is that any visual aid you bring to your presentation has to complement what you're saying in person, not copy it. I find that too many speakers use slides as a crutch because they're not familiar enough with their own material, the flow of their presentation, the key messages they want to include. It always stresses me out when I watch a speaker and they almost seem surprised by their own slides. How is that possible?! Sometimes, slides and visuals are absolutely unavoidable (and I'm about to tell you the cases where I would use them), but they cannot only be something that works for you, they have to also be serving your audience.

Don't just take my word for it – I asked my friend Corey Hajim, the former Business Curator for TED, about slides. 'Slides can break the connection between the speaker and the audience,' she said. 'And I really, honestly and truly believe that a speaker should only have a slide if it's going to show something that can't be explained with words. There are so many times that slides are difficult to understand or complicated and it distracts the audience from what a speaker is trying to say. It's not the intention, but you're working against yourself.'

Now I've spent enough time trash-talking slides, let's move on to the occasions where I think they're completely acceptable. I think visuals need to fall into one of four categories: revelation (where that can be done visually), explanation (which specifically benefits from a visual representation), wonder (to blow the audience's minds with how big or impressive or significant something is visually) and anchoring (to keep your audience on track).

Keep it simple

The key to good slides is to keep them as simple and streamlined as possible. We're talking images, simple graphs that you refer to and contextualise, key phrases rather than full sentences, which you're fleshing out for the audience in person. Your visual content is there to illuminate the content you're sharing verbally, and that verbal element is the main event. Visuals need to serve as a supporting character, not function as a copy-and-paste of what you're saying as a speaker. Something you should consider is that if you make your slides too long and complex, you're then putting them in direct competition with yourself. The audience has to make a choice: do they read your slides and figure out the block of text and context-free graphs, or do they listen to you?

Now, for some industries, the slides are the 'product' that your client expects you to deliver. In this case there's actually a case for making two versions of your slides: one that accompanies your talk, and another that you send via email (potentially in advance). Even if you aren't expected to deliver a report in the form of slides, if it's an important enough presentation, maybe it's one you might have to do more than once, then having two versions of your slide deck could be a good idea. You would create one version where you're the narrator, meaning there's much less text and there's much less explanation needed, and another version where someone reading it wouldn't have the explanation and context of you being in the room.

When making your slides, I recommend settling on a style and using a template that you can reproduce easily. This means choosing one font, or two at most (one for headings, one for body text is fine, and I like to have a specific serif and sans-serif font that I use for everything), and making sure it's big enough for all members of your audience to read. You can use colours to create sections to help guide the audience through the slides and understand where they are in the flow of information. When choosing a colour scheme, I'd recommend running it through a contrast checker for accessibility. These are freely available online and give you feedback on how visible your page would be to someone with impaired vision.

Do sweat the small stuff

If you're using text, I implore you to spell-check it as diligently as if you were turning in an essay. I would even recommend printing it out: something strange happens between the screen and the page and things that your eyes skipped over on your laptop often become glaringly obvious once they hit the physical realm. Can you imagine how silly you'd feel standing in front of a screen and finding out the first slide has a spelling mistake that you could have caught with a bit of time and attention? It's happened to me and I wouldn't recommend it.

There is actually a case for using slides *before* your event. Some speakers find that making a presentation deck with only a few words on each slide helps them with the process of internalisation. The social philosopher Roman Krznaric uses slides as a preparation tool, but the audience often never sees them. 'I'm not saying that everyone should do this, but if I'm giving a twenty-minute keynote, I will make a PowerPoint slide deck for myself,' he told me. 'I will never have more than one slide for every minute and a half. That's my rule. The slides will only have images or maybe a keyword. And I have that in my pocket when I walk on the stage. I never, ever look at it. I haven't memorised exactly what I'm going to say, but I know the slides.'

Whether you use slides as a preparation tool like Roman does, or you choose to use them in your final talk, I want you to think of them as a way to illuminate the material for you and your audience. They don't replace rehearsal time, they don't act as a copy-and-paste of your talk, they couldn't replace *you* on the day. They're there to enhance and enliven the experience, and they should always be *for* the audience. Wherever you land on the slides and visuals, try to never lose sight of that!

Getting useful feedback

Feedback. It's a minefield. Sometimes it feels like you're damned if you do or damned if you don't. Everyone will have their own approaches to feedback based on whether they're the kind of person that will benefit from a lot of information or if that might throw them off, discourage or distract them.

I think the key to finding the right approach to feedback *for you* is to be really specific about what kind of feedback you're looking for, and what you're planning to use it for. And more than anything, remember that you're looking for feedback from the perspective of a *listener*, not a fellow speaker. When we give feedback, we're often doing that based on what we would do as a speaker, rather than thinking about how we would be receiving the content as a member of the audience.

One of my most important pieces of advice on feedback is that not everyone is equally qualified or useful to give it to you. Climate activist Clover Hogan agrees: 'I think I made the mistake early on of seeking feedback from people who weren't very good at giving it in a constructive way. Like, my mom, bless her, her feedback would just be like, "Oh my God, it's amazing. I wouldn't change anything." I'm like "okay, that's not actually that helpful but thank you!" And then my dad would say "Okay. I've rewritten the whole thing. Here's what I think you should say." And fortunately, since then, I've been able to find some amazing mentors for whom this is such a gift, and who appreciate that it is an art, and who also know the art of giving feedback in a way that is genuinely helpful. Because it is such a vulnerable kind of thing, that allows you to take your walls down so that you can receive that feedback.' People in your life may be fundamentally well intentioned but they aren't necessarily going to be able to make your talk or presentation better off the top of their heads.

When I spoke to the comedian Sofie Hagen, they were really clear on the need to protect the core of your work when receiving feedback or criticism on it. 'People will happily give you feedback. The difficult thing is sorting it,' they said. 'You have you, and you have your gut, and you have your art, and you have your story, and you have to cherish and trust that. I feel like a lot of great artists and storytellers started with a lot of people going, *why would you do that?*'

I understand that you might not have access to one-to-one time with an expert in public speaking or in your particular field, and that the only people you do have access to are friends and family. Fear not! That doesn't mean you're adrift at sea without a paddle. Instead, I have a few ways of turning someone who might be inclined to give you unhelpful feedback into someone capable of giving more constructive, applicable comments and critiques, as if by magic.

Ask the right questions

These are the questions I recommend you ask the person you're seeking feedback from to think about *while* they are listening to you. In my experience, I've found they help focus feedback into insights you can actually use without feeling overwhelmed. Remember to tell the person giving you feedback about who your audience is, so they can put themselves in their shoes while they listen.

1. Was it engaging from the very first sentence?

This can give you useful information about your opening and help reassure you that you've figured out the right way to begin. If your opening isn't sparking that curiosity and connection with the audience, how can you make it punchier, spicier, more engaging?

2. Does this make sense? Was anything confusing?

They don't need to be an expert in your subject matter to be able to give you feedback on how you communicated it. Good communication, in theory, means you can make complex ideas digestible to almost anyone. Now, if you're working in a technical or specialist area, you shouldn't expect them to suddenly be intimate with your topic, but they should still have a sense that, in a broad way, they were able to follow the logic of what you were saying. Were they?

3. Were there any impossible leaps?

I get it: sometimes you're so deep in your head that you forget that your audience isn't actually there too. Sometimes you forget to create that connective tissue that links from one idea to the next, or are so enthusiastic about your core message that you leap from one thing to another thing that's actually quite far away from you, without laying down the stepping stones for your audience to get there (remember the analogy I told you about helping your audience to cross the river with the right number and kind of stones? This is the feedback you want here!). Find out if you were taking your audience with you on the journey or you were just wildly leaping into the unknown.

4. Did I use enough or too many examples?

Examples are meant to illustrate and illuminate your point, not overwhelm it. We're focused on ideas, and want to use examples to *prove* that the idea is relevant, possible, solvable. I completely understand the urge to over-example so your audience believes in you and takes your ideas seriously, but sometimes this can be to the detriment of the message. Ask your feedback-helper if they feel the ideas were supported with the right number of relevant examples, or if any of them left them confused.

5. Is the order of the information in the talk correct?

Again, your messy brain holds all the information you want to share and sometimes it doesn't flow out in a way that's *quite* as easy to follow for the audience. You have tonnes of knowledge and context that the audience doesn't have, so this is an opportunity to check that it all flows in a logical order towards the conclusion that your message and your idea is important, and makes the audience want to help you achieve your goals.

6. Was there any unexplained jargon?

I will never forget Corey Hajim, former Business Curator at TED, putting it as simply as 'in every industry, jargon can discredit you'. I couldn't agree more. Find out from your practice audience if you used anything they felt was jargonistic. Maybe the person giving you feedback doesn't know what something means, but you will know whether it's actually 'jargon' or just a specialised word they're unfamiliar with. Now, that doesn't mean you need to remove relevant, specialised language that relates to your area of interest. It means taking a good look at the vocabulary you're using and trying to use language that is the most clear *and* the most accurate at the same time. The right vocabulary for you and your audience will sit in the middle of that Venn diagram.

7. Is it too complex or simplistic?

Again, we want to be finding a sweet spot. Not so high-level that your audience won't follow, but not so simplistic that they'll think you're taking them for a bunch of fools. Did it feel like it was pitched for a curious, engaged, even if non-specialist audience?

8. Did I lose you along the way? Did you notice yourself getting distracted?

I have to credit Chris Anderson, Head of TED, for these questions, because these are possibly *the* biggest questions. It's all very well having an engaging opening, but if that's all you've got, and the rest of it is a bit lacklustre, what was the great opening even for? You've got to structure your talk so there are these continual points of re-engagement, varying the tone, using anecdotes and stories to stop it from feeling like a monotonous barrage of information. Hopefully you'll get some interesting feedback on the moments that need a bit more sparkle, the parts that could do with an example to bring them more vividly to life, and even the really great, juicy bits that you should under no circumstances lose.

9. What did you love?

As human beings we love to focus on the negatives, but it's so important to know what really resonated with your audience or what they enjoyed. This is as much for your confidence as it is to make sure you don't inadvertently take out a good bit while changing what doesn't work! Find out what they would miss if it was removed and don't remove it.

It might feel counter-intuitive to get feedback from people who are not experts in the field, but in the words of environmental activist Pattie Gonia, 'I'm looking for feedback from an audience perspective, not from a performer perspective.'

What to do with feedback

And when you've got all that feedback, are you meant to just completely change your talk or presentation to suit the person making the comments? We've already talked at some length about staying true to yourself, to finding your core message and sharing that with your authentic voice, so it can be hard to take on feedback when it feels that you're being asked to change that. Neil Vora, a science and healthcare communicator specialising in pandemics, told me about finding that balance. 'Over time, I've become more confident about staying true to my authentic self and feeling confident that the message I have, even if someone disagrees, is a fine message to have,' he said. 'But a few things have helped me navigate this over time. One of them is that, a few years ago, I did this programme called the Presidential Leadership Scholars, and one of the most prominent messages that I learned from that experience was to ask myself the question, *Why would a reasonable person think that?* Most people are reasonable and it's okay to disagree, and so just because someone gives some feedback that might not sit with me initially, it's okay for them to have their view, and I can try not to engage with it defensively and try to see the truth in what they're saying.'

It's all about choosing the right person and asking the right questions. I understand the desire to keep your talk close to your chest so you don't feel discouraged by someone's comments, but, on balance, especially if you don't have the experience to know what worked and what didn't in front of an 'actual' audience, it can be so useful to get constructive feedback. Try to do this at a point in the process where – and this is important – you still have time to make changes. It's all about asking the right questions of the right people, and then, once you have real-world experience with *your audience*, you'll have a better idea of how to tailor it in the future, but in absence of that, I think the nine questions I gave you should reap some pretty interesting, actionable comments.

Why I don't believe in 'Impostor Syndrome'

It's easy to get in your head about public speaking. We all know it's something that a lot of people struggle with. If they didn't, I probably wouldn't have a career and you probably wouldn't be reading this book! For many, it's about a fear that they're not an expert, that they don't have the right to be in the room – the assumption that the audience knows more about the topic than they do. But you're there for a reason: because you have something to share, that only you can share in your own personal way.

Now, what about those doubts rearing their ugly head? What about the dreaded 'impostor syndrome'? I have some thoughts on the subject that might help to re-frame the way you think about 'impostor syndrome', and maybe the way you think about yourself.

For a long time, I completely subscribed to the concept of 'impostor syndrome'. I found it so compelling that I actually did quite a lot of research into it, gave two TEDx talks about it and even considered writing a book on the subject. After all, as a millennial woman, it's become an almost-universal part of how we think about ourselves and how we engage with the world.

The origins of 'impostor syndrome'

'Impostor syndrome' was first discussed in 1978 in the journal *Psychotherapy Theory, Research and Practice* by two academics at Georgia State University – Pauline Rose Clance and Suzanne Imes. They worked specifically with high-achieving women and found that many of them had 'a strong belief that they are not intelligent; in fact they are convinced that they have fooled anyone who thinks otherwise' and they had a 'fear that eventually some significant person will discover that they are indeed intellectual impostors.'

So what changed? Why did I stop believing in 'impostor syndrome', and why do I not want to engage with it in the context of this book? For me, it was this growing sense that the problem wasn't a unique phenomenon, wasn't a personal insecurity that we could be coached out of. It became more and more clear to me that, in most cases, 'impostor syndrome' is actually a completely rational response to a culture that values some people more than others, that gives some a seat at the table while leaving others out in the cold. Why *wouldn't* someone feel like an impostor when they know, through their own experience, that spaces are not designed with them in mind? Why wouldn't someone feel like an impostor when their expertise is treated as if it's insignificant because it corresponds to a different kind of knowledge than the Western canon?

It may not be surprising that I held on to the notion of 'impostor syndrome' as long as I did, given that I felt it had been such a major factor in my life.

When my family moved from London to New York as a child, I went from being an A-student in London to failing in New York. I was in a whole new environment, a whole new school system, and I just couldn't maintain my previous grades. I was a fish out of water. Repeatedly failing to distinguish myself as a good student when I previously had been extremely capable was especially difficult when it came to applying to universities. I didn't aim for top universities and ended up getting an average SAT score, which by that point I had convinced myself I deserved. It came as a shock when I got accepted into a top Canadian university where I had applied on a whim. I convinced myself it must be a mistake on their part, sheer luck, or that the university wasn't actually that prestigious after all. Towards the end of my psychology degree, I applied to be in a child and adolescent depression lab as an undergraduate researcher. It was very competitive, and yet I made it through the two rounds of interviews. Once I was accepted, I still had to pass a test that most people fail on their first try, so I decided to try it with very little preparation, just to see what it was like before studying for my second attempt. I passed the first time. Anyone would feel proud of that, right? Not me. I felt like I'd lied my way through not only my interviews, but now my exam too. This feeling of being a cheat, or even an *impostor*, led me to believe I really didn't know what I was doing and consequently I stopped attending the meetings and training and I eventually left the lab having done only a tiny fraction of the work I was definitely capable of doing. When I would talk about my career, it would often revolve around luck, chance, or other people giving me a break. I would never credit my own hard work with being the reason that that luck came about or why I, specifically, would be the person someone would give a break to.

It didn't occur to me then that I might feel out of place or less deserving of a seat at the table because I was a woman of colour who had to work and take out loans to put myself through university. I put it all on myself, without considering that I was operating in a deeply racist and sexist culture that judges the value of women in particular on their appearance. It seems obvious to me now that much of what we attribute to 'impostor syndrome' is simply seeing the world for what it is.

On top of the things I experienced in my own life, the 'impostor syndrome' situation really spiked for me when I first started approaching people to do TEDx talks as part of my role in TEDxLondon and TEDxLondonWomen. I would invite people who I had researched and identified as great potential speakers, whether they were upcoming talents or already well established in their field of work. But time and time again, when they would get back to me, instead of jumping at the opportunity to share their knowledge with a willing and engaged audience, their responses would be riddled with anxiety. They would be questioning their own abilities and expertise, the very same abilities and expertise that had drawn me to them in the first place. This was more common with women I contacted but was certainly not limited to them. I would hear things like 'I'm not an expert', 'I'm not good enough to give a TEDx talk', 'I wouldn't know what to say' and so on. Sometimes I was able to push through these doubts and, with my support, we would develop an excellent talk, proving that they had nothing to worry about in the first place. All of this I put down to 'impostor syndrome', but I now recognise it as the logical outcome of structural exclusion and factors such as sexism, racism, ableism and more.

If we think back to the women from Clance and Imes's study which coined the term, we can see a more logical explanation. Now, with the hindsight of several decades of sociological study, it should be quite clear to anyone that the problem in this situation was sexism, not the women's own low opinions of themselves. It was almost certainly sexism that had excluded these women from positions of authority and prevented them from having their skills and knowledge recognised.

Esha Bhandari, one of my oldest friends and a human rights lawyer, had an interesting perspective on how she's outgrown 'impostor syndrome'. 'I've always loved public speaking, but I had a lot of fear of exposure, that I'd be exposed as not knowing what I'm talking about, or someone would ask me a question I don't have the answer to,' she told me. 'And the nice thing about being at a different stage in my career and having more experience is that those fears don't land in the same way. One, because I have more experience, so I feel like I do know what I'm talking about. And then, two, I also have enough experience to know that if there's a question I don't know the answer to, it's okay to say that, and it's not a reflection on me, because I do know a lot of things and I do have a lot of substantive experience and things to share and convey.'

So, let's think about 'impostor syndrome' again. Do you have 'impostor syndrome', or are you capable of recognising the deeply entrenched biases that have caused you to question yourself? Is the reason that you're questioning your ability to perform in a public-speaking scenario because you're Black, or you're a woman, or you're using a mobility aid, or your first language isn't English? Or maybe even all of the above? Because, if so, I totally get it. In our culture, certain types of knowledge are prized above others, certain faces are prized above others, certain bodies are prized above others, certain accents are prized above others. It's not surprising that you could feel like you don't belong.

Reframing what makes you different

But the reason you're reading this book and the reason you're about to embark on public speaking is precisely *because* you have something to say that no one else can say for you. It is unique to you, and that is your particular strength. You have expertise that no one else possesses, purely by virtue of being you. Don't think of yourself in an abstract way in the context of your field of study or area of work, just think of yourself specifically in the context of this speaking engagement. You are the only person who could deliver this particular talk, because you are the only person who could write this particular material, because you are the only person with this knowledge and this voice and this style.

If you've absorbed all that and you know you have every right to be here, but you're still feeling those physical nerves, that's okay! That's totally normal. Our bodies are mysterious beasts and we can't always control them. I know it's the most basic trick in the book but breathing exercises really do help, so it could be helpful to take a second before you begin to just have some quiet time and take a breath. There are lots of different approaches to breathing, but any technique that means you're taking long, slow, deep breaths will be better for you than letting your breathing run away with your thoughts. Even the simple act of breathing in for six seconds and holding it before breathing out for six seconds will help to get your body feeling more relaxed and ready for the stage. Maybe you should think about doing this anyway, even if you don't *think* you feel nervous, and especially if you're speaking to a big group at a large venue, so that it doesn't hit you all of a sudden when you get onstage. All I'm saying is there are worse ways to waste time than by doing breathing exercises you might not need.

Why you shouldn't 'fake it til you make it'

You often see advice to 'fake it til you make it', and it's not that it's *wrong*, because if it works for you then great, but I always find it risky. This is doubly true for people who think they're suffering from 'impostor syndrome', because you're building your whole house on a shaky foundation rather than figuring out what's making it shaky in the first place. It can never *really* be a long-term solution to your problem, but I understand why it's tempting in the moment.

I can't help you fake confidence, and I don't particularly want to either, but I hope I can help you think in a more useful way about things that are *real*, whether it's structural exclusion, your own experience, your accent. I hope I can remind you that your voice is valuable, that your knowledge is powerful, that if you've historically been excluded from spaces and opportunities, it's not your fault and you're not an impostor. I hope that in the process of planning, assembling and delivering your talk, you realise just how special your personal perspective and expertise are, and that you deserve to be there just as much as anybody else.

> Jodie Jackson, an expert on training your brain for well-being and peak performance, has shared some wise words that might help when the nerves set in. She calls it *rewiring* or *reprogramming*, to help your brain co-operate with the task you have to overcome:

Maryam Pasha

Your mind is a muscle, and if you're struggling with nerves, it's to do with your psychology, and your psychology can be retrained. One of the activities that can help retrain your psychology is just to change the way you speak about yourself.

Don't say *I'm nervous, I'm shy, I'm this, I'm that*. Whatever word you're going to use to describe yourself, make it phenomenal. A formula that I'd use when you're creating your identity statement is 'I am adjective + noun'. So, an adjective like incredible, inspiring, magnetic, passionate, wonderful, powerful. Plus a noun like speaker, leader, coach, whatever it is.

If you don't believe it, or you can't think of the words for who you might be as a speaker, find a few speakers that you admire. Find what you love about them, and make a note of that. Are they funny? Are they compassionate? Are they passionate?

Focus in on the qualities that you like, because we're all going to like different things. What qualities do they have that really draw you to them, or that you admire about them? Then you can take those attributes, steal them, and then become them.

If you *really* can't resist comparing yourself to other people, please do remember that comparing a messy, unpolished, first draft of your talk to a TED talk that's had fifteen million views is never going to be helpful. No one is expecting that of you, and you can't see any of the work that went into getting it there. Odds are, once upon a time that talk was in exactly the same state yours is, because no one – and I mean *no one* – is able to just cough up a shiny, flawless talk fully-formed on day one. You have no idea how many times they've given a version of that presentation, how much refinement has gone into honing the ideas, the language, the stories, the cadence, how many hours of rehearsal, how much feedback they've taken on board. If you're willing to do the same, and give your talk or presentation what it needs to make it as good as it can possibly be, *then* we can talk about comparing them. But until then, absolutely not!

When you give in to the idea of 'impostor syndrome', you're letting the negative voices win and you're not sharing the stories and ideas that might just move the needle. You want to speak because these messages are important to you and because you believe in the idea of change. That's what needs to win right now, not the status quo, and you're just the person to do it.

Section 4

Common Questions Answered

In this section, I'll be teaming up with several of the experts you've already heard from throughout the book to explore key questions about storytelling and public speaking that you might have, whether you're a nervous first-time speaker or an experienced communicator, giving a wedding speech or a TEDx talk.

Do I need to do anything differently when I speak online?

There's no escaping it: speaking online is, in the delivery sense, a different beast to speaking in person. Whatever the size of the audience, it brings its own challenges and is in many ways more difficult than real-life speaking.

It's tempting to dive straight into your content, but I would recommend giving a moment to let everyone settle in. 'It's like going into a restaurant, sitting down and, literally, they serve you a steak. Hang on a minute. Can I look at the menu? Can I have sparkling water? Can I have a glass of orange juice? An amuse-bouche is there for a reason,' says public speaking expert Simon Bucknall.

Let's start with the basics. When you're speaking to someone in person, you would look at them and make eye contact. Next time you're in an online meeting (Zoom, Teams, etc), I want you to notice where you're looking when you speak. Looking at the person on screen or even directly into your camera might not mean the person on the other end feels like you're looking at them. I've found that for my set-up I have to focus on a point directly below my camera, in the top 20% of my screen, to make eye contact and speak directly to people. I suggest testing this out – make a recording of yourself looking at different places on your screen and camera to find out what is best. What you absolutely want to avoid is your camera being on one device and the screen you view being on another, so you are always facing the wrong direction.

For me personally, one of the most vital parts of public speaking is getting live feedback from the audience, reading the room and responding with my body language, voice, movement, all of that. Obviously, that is much harder to achieve with delivering online workshops and content, when the audience isn't physically in the room with you.

I would recommend you voice record yourself delivering your content and play it back. See how you feel when you listen to it, and try to detach yourself from the fact you know the material inside out. Listen with the ears of a person who's hearing it for the first time. Do you feel energised? Awake? Engaged? Or are you switching off? You need to bring a lot more energy to delivering online content. You need to bring the enthusiasm because you can't guarantee it from your audience, especially online. You are carrying it for everyone, which, I know, is a lot of pressure, but with sufficient energy, it can be done! It can feel particularly weird to do this online because odds are, you're broadcasting live from your living room, office or a little soundproofed booth, not from a stage. Your impulse will be to bring down the energy level to the physical space you're in, but I need you to overcome that and take everything to a bigger, bolder, louder and more assertive place.

Given that there are a lot of drawbacks of speaking online, it's even more important to use the assets available too. 'What you miss is that ability to read the room, so you have to build it into the session and create tangible opportunities for people to do that. I structure my content in a way that there are continual re-engagement points throughout,' says Ben Hurst. 'Online, those things are usually questions, chatboxes, opportunities to enter some data to make sure people are still awake and paying attention. I like putting people into small groups with really clear instructions about what I want them to talk about for ninety seconds and then bringing them back.' And it's important to start these engagements *early*, rather than structuring it so you're speaking at the audience for a long period, and then they engage at the end. You want to set their expectations so they understand they'll be expected to engage, if not contribute, so they're more likely to be actively listening rather than letting their attention wander or sneakily checking their emails. As Simon says: 'The longer they remain inactive, the harder it becomes to activate!'

Enabling that activity might require a little bit of preparation and checking in with the person who booked you ahead of time. Roman Krznaric advises planning ahead so you know you'll be able to engage with the audience in the ways you want to: 'I ask the organisers or the tech people, can you set up a camera so it's looking at the audience, so I can see the audience and I can see them responding. I spoke at a conference for NASA space scientists the other day – they're in Arizona, I'm in Oxford. They're in some weird conference centre and it's eight o'clock in the morning, and I'm a giant face on a screen, so I asked to see the audience and then asked them to wave so I knew they were really there!' This might seem like a small thing, but just having this understanding that both parties can see each other can be a good start for keeping everyone engaged and attentive.

My boss has asked me to start presenting at work and I don't want to mess it up. Help!

Fundamentally, presenting in a business setting is no different to any other kind of public speaking: you still need to make it gripping and compelling and engaging for your audience. Just because you're presenting research or data doesn't mean that everything you know about public speaking and storytelling should go out the window.

Cognitive economist Leigh Caldwell told me that, psychologically, people have structures in their minds by which they understand and navigate the environment they're in, and these are called schemas. 'One example of a schema is in an airport. You kind of know that in an airport you're going to arrive, you'll be dropped off, you'll check your bags in, you go through security, you'll sit in the lounge for a bit, you get on the plane. Everyone knows where they are in that process and what's just happened and what's happening next. That's the same with people consuming information. If they have a schema that tells them, *here's the structure of what you're hearing, here's what you're expecting to hear next, here's how it all fits together,* this makes it much more understandable as well as much more memorable. You don't get lost in the middle, and it's much harder to get distracted.' Think about how you can structure and signpost your content to keep people actively listening and aware of where they are in your presentation.

I've made clear many, many times that audience is key to good communication, and knowing your audience is both easier and harder when the audience is just one person or even just a few people. You might have assumed you know what they need from you or what background information they already have, but it can still be valuable to have an extra chat or gather more information about them ahead of time. Although sometimes *getting* that time is easier said than done!

One of the most common dynamics in business presentations is pitching for investment. If we want to get semi-philosophical here, it's reasonable to say that we bring various assumptions to presentations like this: for example, that the investor might be sceptical from the beginning. That's because we all have our own stories already in our minds, and maybe they've told themselves they're the noble guardians of this money and you're the cunning raider trying to part them from it. But it's important to remember that this isn't the only story you could tell about this relationship. If you think about the people you're pitching to as the protagonist in their own story, what would be the best way to frame and think about the potential relationship between them, their investment and you or your project?

There's one really good reason to consider storytelling in business presentations: audiences are *distracted*. Your presence is standing between them and their phones, their emails, their next meeting. Sure, it's rude, but it's just the way of the world these days. The reason they are spending time on other activities is that they are not convinced your presentation is valuable enough to them to justify their attention. So it's on you to convince them! Grab their attention with a good story or a curiosity-provoking opening. But as a backup, make sure you state your key points at the beginning, repeat them at least once in the middle, and again at the end. Then even your most distracted audience has several chances to get the point.

If it doesn't feel appropriate for you to use storytelling on a big scale, like structuring your presentation as The Hero's Journey, you can still think about storytelling within the presentation. Good stories have cause and effect, they have characters, they have conflict. Your presentation doesn't need to be a list of facts you're relaying to the audience! Leigh Caldwell recalls a particularly flat presentation he had seen, and explains why: 'There was no obvious reason why slide ten came after slide nine. You want to know why this piece of information is coming now, and why it didn't come before, and why it doesn't come after. Everything should be at an almost inevitable place in the order.' This idea of cause and effect should help you figure out the most engaging way to break down your data or your research in a way that keeps the audience locked in.

I think it's also important to remember that not every storytelling structure or convention will be totally right for presenting in business meetings. Some are better than others, and Problem-Solution is often great in these contexts: you've told your audience about a problem the business is facing, and then there's a natural, simple flow to the solution. And while a surprise ending may be delightful in the cinema, it might not be great for a presentation, especially if you've laid out and signposted what the logical next step should be.

When it comes to presenting at work, there's a temptation to completely erase yourself from the situation. Maybe it's because you're concerned people will think you're showing off, or boasting, or angling for a promotion. I think people in the U.K. are particularly guilty of this! While I'm not suggesting you go full TV presenter-mode, if you think about it from the point of view of serving your audience, they are best served by something that's engaging and memorable, and it's completely fine if your personality traits become part of that. We worry that we're not being 'professional' enough, but you want to make sure that even in these situations, you're incorporating your unique insights, your personality, your experiences and your perspectives in a way that makes it as compelling as possible.

In some businesses you may have a template you're supposed to follow for certain kinds of presentations. If you can avoid following the template, you'll have more room for telling a story that suits the message and the audience. But even if you can't, you can still innovate within its constraints: for example, show a slide of data but tell a story verbally over the top of it. Make your presence essential to carrying the presentation, not an unnecessary addition to it.

I've never done public speaking before and I'm really nervous. How do I get over it?

I totally get feeling nervous when you've never done something before. It's strange, it's unfamiliar, you don't know what's going to happen. But here's the thing: I still get nervous. This is basically my whole job, and I still feel the same anxieties you're facing right now. For me, it kicks in about thirty minutes before I have to go on stage or deliver a workshop to a new group or have my first coaching call with a new client. I'm absolutely overwhelmed by the thought that 'this is a terrible idea! Why did I agree to do this! It would have been easier to just stay in bed today!' The researcher and storyteller Brené Brown calls this 'FFT' or 'F*cking First Time'. It's a concept she uses to describe the experience of doing something new, challenging or vulnerable, acknowledging the inherent discomfort and uncertainty that comes with it.

Mostly what you're feeling (heart pounding, butterflies in your stomach, sweating) is the physical experience of adrenaline, and that's okay! Just let yourself feel it, even if it's not a pleasant sensation for you. The first part of the battle is to *not* fight it. Just accept that these things are happening, and will probably continue to happen to you when you speak in the future, and try to make friends with it as best you can.

In the words of Corey Hajim, the former Business Curator for TED: 'I often just tell people, look, being nervous is normal and human, and what you just have to remember is, *I can do the thing while being nervous*. We do lots of things while we're nervous. And you know you're gonna be nervous walking on the stage, and then once you get going you can start to relax.'

I can do the thing while being nervous. That is such a powerful and true statement and I want you to carry that with you every time you start to doubt yourself.

Try to think of this as an amazing opportunity to share what you have to say with the world . . . or at least a few people! My friend Jodie Jackson, who is a neuro-encoding specialist, is a fan of creating an 'identity statement' for yourself as a speaker, and I would definitely recommend this to someone who's speaking for the first time. Think of a sentence that starts 'I am' and is followed by an adjective, then a noun, and then a verb that all encapsulate what you're hoping to achieve, who you're trying to be. So a verb like 'I am an incredible/inspiring/magnetic/passionate/powerful/knowledgeable' followed by, in your case, the word 'speaker' as the noun, though maybe on another day it might be 'leader' or 'writer' or 'friend', then whatever it is that you want to do with your talk. Maybe 'that empowers people' or 'that changes lives' or 'transforms the world' or 'creates new ways of thinking'. Whatever fits your purpose and your identity, and hopefully turns this from a scary moment into something that feels like an incredible opportunity to do good.

And I know I've covered it before (multiple times!), but I'm going to say it again: prepare, prepare, prepare. Practise until you have the *real* confidence to carry it off. Practise until you know it backwards. The best way to feel on top of your material when you've never delivered it before is to be so intimately acquainted with it that it's second nature to you. That way, even if nerves do set in, they're less likely to get the better of you because you *know* you're the master of your content. As my friend and TED speaker Vidhya Ramalingam says, 'Over-prepare, just for the sake of it. Over-prepare to whatever level is right for you to feel comfortable and confident going in. And whatever that level is might look different for each person, but even if it means, write out every single word you're going to say, and if you're moderating, write out every single question you might ask, write it all out.' That's your superpower. Not just the confidence, but the preparation.

Being nervous is so normal that people who have spoken in front of big audiences hundreds of times still feel it too. Sarah Ellis, who co-founded Amazing If and Squiggly Careers, is a very experienced speaker, and yet she gets nervous. 'I get really nervous going on live radio. That's my little nemesis – I don't like the fact they can ask you about anything,' she told me. 'So I write down three words that I want to use to describe how I'm going to show up in that interview. So it might be "calm, optimistic and useful", and they're not always exactly the same words, but I use that all the time whenever I am nervous about speaking. They're my words that I can connect with, and they stop me trying to be all things for people. If I do those three things, if I'm calm, optimistic and useful, then that's a job well done.' The idea of taking back control of a situation where you feel like you don't have much control can be really powerful.

If you're really feeling unsure of whether your talk is working, I would strongly recommend heading back to the 'feedback' section and seeking feedback *exclusively* using the list of questions I gave you there. When you're nervous, you're probably also feeling vulnerable and sensitive, and this puts you in a position where you might change things that you shouldn't change because you feel like you might as well do *something*. Sticking within the realms of useful feedback will hopefully give you a bit of reassurance that you're on the right track, or highlight where you could get that little extra bit of confidence. Again, we want the confidence to be real, to be based in something, to be based on your skills and knowledge and hard work. You're nervous because you care, and likewise, you've done the work because you care.

But don't just take my word for it: Kumi Naidoo, who was head of Greenpeace so knows a thing or two about speaking to large audiences, confirms this. 'Every speech I give I'm nervous,' he told me. 'That nervous energy helps you never to take an audience for granted. Secondly, it helps you remind yourself that every audience is different.'

Remember: the more you do it, the less significant each individual case will feel when it doesn't go to plan, partly because you have the data to show that it *can* go well and you *can* speak successfully. Experienced public speaker, civil liberties lawyer Esha Bhandari puts it like this: 'When you're doing it frequently, so much less rides on that one time. If you do this once in a blue moon and it's not your best time, then it can affect your confidence. I do it often enough that I can be like, *You know what? That was not my best day, that did not go well, I didn't do these things, but it's fine because I've had other days where I've done well, and I will have future days where I get to do it again.*' Keeping perspective is really vital!

How do I use public speaking and storytelling to advocate for the environment (and other complex issues)?

There aren't many areas of communication that feel more high-stakes than the climate. It's something that a lot of my work focuses on and that I care about. I wrote this section thinking specifically about climate change, but as someone who also worked in human rights and refugee rights for almost a decade, I think the ideas here also apply to other issues where you might be trying to have a positive impact in your community and the world.

One person who has taught me so much about climate and climate communication is Clover Hogan: 'The thing that really struck me in the climate movement was that the science was so alarming and terrifying, but it was so difficult to actually make sense as a regular person of what is happening. So I really saw a gap for myself as an activist in this space, to help translate some of that science and that jargon and put it in terms that people not just understood, but in terms that would actually connect to them on an emotional level, in a way that really shifted the way they saw the world and also how they saw their own role in it.'

In such a huge all-encompassing area like climate, focus becomes even more vital. Your talk or presentation *still* needs that one idea, that message, that one single core objective, even when you're talking about a topic as broad as climate change. You want your audience to leave you feeling motivated to do something differently, to take a specific action, to join you in campaigning around a particular issue, rather than to nebulously just 'care more' about the climate. Stay laser-focused on that, and your audience is more likely to come along with you.

But it's also important not to lose sight of your own sense of self and sense of purpose: for some climate communicators, the idea of meeting people where they're at (which is broadly a good thing) can feel like it conflicts with their goals. It's about trying to craft your communication in such a way that it aligns with your values *and* achieves the desired effect you're looking for. Clover told me that, when she started out, she tried to take what she calls a 'Trojan horse approach' of cloaking the things she cared about in language she thought her audience would understand. But, over time, she started to feel as if she was doing herself and her message a disservice and damaging her integrity, because, in her words, she was 'trying to squeeze climate into a hole that didn't fit'. 'I think, with time, I learned it's not so much about trying to squeeze it into a jargon they'll understand but treating whoever you're speaking to as a human being, acknowledging the challenges they're up against.'

In this way, it's got a lot to do with the ideas back in the sections on audience: knowing what your core message is, and knowing how to adapt *how* you talk about it, not *what* you're talking about, will help you keep that balance of integrity around climate communications versus meeting your audience where they're at.

Any kind of scientific communication can be challenging, especially when trying to share ideas that might feel abstract or out of reach for many people. Jonathan Foley is an environmental scientist, TED speaker and Executive Director of Project Drawdown. He comes from a rigorously scientific background, but knows that there's no reason to squeeze all the humanity and grace out of science while still presenting it truthfully and on its own terms. 'When I think of really good science communication, I always think of Carl Sagan. There's just something about the clarity of language, the use of metaphor, the use of relatable examples, and decluttering of jargon is a prerequisite for good, scientific communication that can be not only clear, but even inspiring. He doesn't tell personal stories about his childhood or people he loves, or great icons of the world. But still, it's moving and stirs the soul, because he evokes awe and wonder, which are other really important emotional chords to strike.'

Science journalist and Climate Curator at TED David Biello told me that he thinks the days of the 'information deficit' model around climate comms are over. There used to be a belief that if we just provided people with the facts and the right information that they would change their minds and become engaged in climate activism. 'Most people have heard of climate change and have an opinion,' he told me. 'Reciting a list of statistics or other facts and figures or history or whatever else you might fall back on for that information deficit model is not going to work at all. What does seem to work is trusted messengers.' Making sure you're communicating authentically, accurately and authoritatively will help to make you one of those trusted messengers.

I think climate change in particular is an area where it's valuable to not just be a speaker, but to also be an audience member as much as possible. When the stakes are *so* high, it falls to all of us to work together for the common goal of taking better care of our one planet. What can you learn from other speakers in your area of interest? And I don't even necessarily mean in person: on the TED website alone, there's a treasure trove of climate and environmental talks. What do *you* find motivating in the speakers? How do they leave you feeling energised to do the work? What are the techniques they're using to make the issue feel accessible to the audience without compromising on the integrity of their message? It's not about copying what they're saying, it's about looking for common threads in climate change communication that you feel are effective at getting the vital work done.

I think all of this is also true for other complex issues. When I wrote this section I was thinking about climate change specifically, but, on reflection, everything I've said here could equally apply to other complex or wicked problems.

Can I really change the world with a story?

There's actually a specific category of public speaking known as 'impact storytelling' that refers to this exact situation. You could argue that many different kinds of speaking fall under 'impact storytelling', but this is about taking a human-centred approach to problems, and creating change. Most of the people I've spoken to for this book could be described as impact storytellers, because they're generally speaking with a desire to change systems. But how do they use public speaking to achieve that?

When we're thinking about taking a 'human-centred' approach, it can feel obvious that trying to provoke the very human emotion of empathy is the way forward, but Nathalie McDermott thinks differently. As Nathalie is the founder and co-CEO of Heard, a narrative change organisation working to shift how social issues are portrayed in popular culture, I had a lot of questions for her on the subject of impact storytelling! 'Empathy is useful,' she says, 'but for us campaign communicators, it doesn't work as well as we think it does. For example, depictions of how awful the act of abuse is might create empathy in a person, but we still find ways to distance ourselves from that reality, like it couldn't happen to me. It's similar with migration, the classic thing of photos of people in boats. You just think, *I feel sorry for those poor people, but I wouldn't have done that, I wouldn't put my kid on a boat, here are all the ways that this doesn't apply to me.* So the job of communicators is to marry that sense of urgency with a sense of efficacy.' By efficacy, Nathalie means the idea that there's something we can do. That's what being an impact storyteller is all about: not just telling the audience about terrible things that are happening in the world and hoping that's enough, but equipping them with the information and the motivation to help contribute to the solution.

It also doesn't mean piling on graphic images or intense stories and believing that will motivate your audience to change. 'We can only take so much horror as humans before we either go numb and stop feeling anything, or we just run a mile,' Nathalie added. You have to be crafting a compelling talk or presentation, using story and narrative structure, bringing in tonal variety, sprinkling in some surprising and interesting data, keeping the audience on their toes and their mind engaged. You can't rely on shock value and sheer force of will and call it impact storytelling.

Again, it goes back to something we talked about in the section on how to make your audience care. Nathalie put it this way: 'I think we, as campaigners, we are very passionate. Often we're scared, angry or concerned about the problem, and that's what's brought us to working on that problem in the first place. But we are unintentionally handing that fear, anger, frustration over to our audiences, because we want to share the problem. We want people to get on board. But of course, it does the opposite.'

Think about the word 'impact'. You're storytelling because you want your words, your story to have an impact. Creating a situation where your audience is essentially frozen in a fight-or-flight response to your content because it's so stressful and distressing is the opposite of what you're trying to achieve. This is why being clear on what you actually want from your audience will help with your impact storytelling. We're going to hear a lot more from campaigner Payzee Mahmod in the next section on personal storytelling, but her clarity of purpose will really help here with the idea of storytelling for change: 'When I spoke to people at the UN, I realised they're super high profile, they don't have time to listen to me go on and on, so I kept it super straightforward and digestible. I said, *this is the problem, I lived it, I know the solutions, here is one solution that can scale globally, and this is how you can help, so what are we waiting for?* I think simplifying your information, making it really bite size and offering a solution are key.'

The idea of a solution doesn't mean you need to have all the building blocks in place to create a different reality all by yourself. It does mean that you need to be able to guide your audience through the story and at least propose some kind of solution, offer some kind of way forward, suggest the actions that you are personally taking in order to see this different world become real. When we talk about 'offering solutions', it doesn't mean that you personally will be able to stop the deforestation of the Amazon or end animal testing, but your audience should be able to walk away from your talk with a sense of purpose, of tangible things they can do with the information that you've shared. You need to think about what power or influence your audience has, and how to use that in service of your goal.

The social philosopher Roman Krznaric, whose work focuses on creating social change, made a really important point about impact storytelling: *you* might have given this particular talk fifty times, but your audience has never heard it before. 'You need to remember that and respect them. You've got to tell it to them like they've never heard it, and you cannot sound bored.' I'm hopeful that you're so passionate and engaged in your message and your content that there isn't a chance that you'll sound bored, but it seems worth reminding you that just because this content isn't new to you, it's still brand new to your audience.

Impact storytelling can be an area where facts and data are extremely useful. Asking your audience to imagine a world where things are done differently can be made more palatable with the data that shows such a world is possible. It's a beautiful goal, to want your audience to walk out of the room believing in change, and if you construct your talk right, it's completely possible.

Sophie Williams, anti-racism advocate and author of *The Glass Cliff* (2024), knows the power of using storytelling to try to shift the needle on the issues that are important to her.

I know that as someone who looks younger than I am, who is non-white, who is a woman, who is neurodivergent, I have to have a really good and unshakable basis in what I'm saying for people to take me seriously, for people to believe me, for people to listen to me.

And I guess it comes back to storytelling. I could tell you about things that have happened in my life, or things that happened that I've observed, but the experience for the majority of my professional life was, when recounting those, just not being believed or being told, 'This is a you thing', or 'This didn't happen', or 'I'm sure they didn't mean it that way'. So the best way that I have found to be able to advocate for myself is to know that I have the data and the information, and not just at a singular level, but at a group level, to say, 'Not only did this happen, this happens on a much wider scale than you imagine, but you don't recognise that because it doesn't happen to you. And because you are from a group, generally, who is used to being believed and you don't perceive me as being part of that group; here is the really robust data that I can give you that backs that up.'

When I read the research papers that relate to areas of things that I'm interested in, it doesn't feel difficult for me to see the themes there, or to pull together the threads, because I'm not being told something I don't believe. It's more, to me, finally seeing the evidence and the proof that I can use to back up that story that I want to tell to be believed. And so I don't really have a struggle with taking that and translating it, because it seems so clear to me from the beginning.

How do I tell a difficult personal story?

I've tried to make clear that storytelling does not always mean telling personal stories from your life, and yet... sometimes it does. It's absolutely not out of the question that if you've had unusual or extreme experiences, that they will form part of your storytelling arsenal.

But remember: no public speaking opportunity will be worth giving away parts of yourself you're not ready to give. There will be ways to communicate the message you're trying to share without telling your audience things you aren't comfortable telling. You should always feel in control of your personal story, and any time you feel that you're being coerced to divulge personal information, or to amplify the traumatic elements of your story, that should be a big red flag that someone might not have your best interests at heart.

Some stories are just unavoidably difficult, and if you do feel ready to share them, it's really important to keep checking in with yourself and making sure you're feeling in control. Feeling emotional is not in itself a red flag that you're not ready to share your story, or that you're going to be sharing it in an unprofessional way. It's not about suppressing your emotions or sugar-coating your experiences, it's more about whether or not you can tell your story with intention and use those emotions in service of your message or goal. 'You have to experience the emotion, then you have to learn to get the emotion under control, and then you have to learn to release the emotion in a controlled way,' says Ben Hurst.

Someone with a huge amount of experience in personal storytelling is Payzee Mahmod, who campaigns to end child marriage and so-called 'honour-based' abuse. The reason she's such a passionate advocate for these causes is because she's lived them. As part of her campaigning, Payzee has shared her story of being forced to marry a thirty-year-old man when she was a child, at just sixteen. She also speaks about the murder of her sister Banaz by their father, uncle and three other men from their community. It goes without saying that both of these are incredibly traumatic experiences. As part of a decade-long battle to change the age of marriage around the world, Payzee has chosen to tell these stories repeatedly. And she has been successful in raising the legal age of marriage to eighteen in England and Wales, something that would have changed the path of her own life.

The key to personal storytelling is to dispense your story and the difficult things that go along with it *strategically*. Payzee puts it like this: 'My biggest advice to people would be that if you want longevity in telling your story and having an impact, then storytelling that shocks ten thousand people once is not as effective as actually moving five people every single time you talk. I have seen the long term impact of that.' Shocking people is not the reason you're telling your story – your purpose is to engage your audience to create change.

Trusting yourself to be an expert with your own story is really important. It's your own life you're talking about, and you have both the right and the ability to share that in the way that feels right to you. Payzee remembers me telling her this when we were working together on her talk for TEDxLondonWomen, 'A survivor's plea to end child marriage'. 'You used to always say to me, *Payzee, you are the expert in your story*, and I go with that feeling, not in any big-headed way, but that I know what I'm talking about because I've lived it. I know the problem and I know the solution, and it's only if you've actually lived through something that you can offer the right solutions.' I think that's crucial: much like with impact storytelling, personal storytelling is *also* about helping the audience find solutions to the problems you're sharing with them. It's not just about telling them a really distressing story and walking away, you're using that story in order to move the needle and bring about change.

Hidden within that piece of advice from Payzee is something I really want to highlight: you don't have to do this alone. Payzee was working with me on her TEDx talk, so she already had someone built into the process to bounce ideas off, someone to ask questions and check in with. You won't always be in that situation where there's a specific person or point of contact helping you craft your talk, but that doesn't mean you can't ask for help. I find that campaigners and people who want to change things are often held back by the belief they have to do everything on their own, and that people who change the world are just magic, singular beings who don't need help. I think that's a really harmful myth. It is so valuable for you to have a trusted person that you can run things by, so you can talk things over when you get in your own head or wonder if you're sharing the wrong things.

Something I really want to make clear is that just because it's *your personal story*, it doesn't mean you can skip all the legwork that goes into crafting a talk or presentation. If anything, it makes it all the more important, because you don't want to use your emotional energy on something that isn't going to resonate with your audience because you didn't construct it and prepare it enough. 'You need to know your story inside out,' Payzee confirmed to me. 'Before I did my TEDx talk, I was going into rooms where I definitely did not know my story inside out because I hadn't said it enough and wasn't confident in my story.' Your storytelling will get so much more effective and impactful if you are intimately familiar with your material, and effective and impactful is absolutely what you're aiming for.

How do I prepare for a TED or TEDx talk?

Of course, as the curator of TEDxLondon, I feel like I could write a whole book on TED and TEDx talks alone, but I'll try to keep this concise! To be honest, everything in this book can be applied to being a TEDx speaker, so I would recommend trying to take in as much of it as you can, but there are a few elements that are TEDx-specific.

Firstly, it's a huge opportunity and I hope you're feeling really excited about it. As a curator, I'm looking for people whose talks have the potential to change the way people understand the world, the way they feel about an issue or change their behaviour – or some combination of those three. The point of a TEDx talk is to make expertise accessible: taking complex ideas and turning them into something that anyone can engage with. The goal for a TEDx speaker should not just be 'to be a TEDx speaker', but to share your message with as many people as possible through this platform.

When thinking about what you want to talk about, focus on ideas that are generous, that are worth spreading, that benefit the world. The best TEDx speakers, in my experience, are not on stage because they love speaking. They're on stage because they have something to say and they know that idea is more powerful than any fear or self-consciousness they might experience. Spend a lot of time figuring out your message. That should be the north star or throughline that determines all the other choices you make while putting your TEDx talk together. Go back to the section 'What is your big idea?' and take my advice on getting messy, on spending time talking to people, having conversations around your area of interest, until you figure out what it is you're really trying to say.

One of the most crucial parts of being a TEDx speaker is being familiar with the format. I would absolutely not recommend starting to craft your TEDx talk without having watched at least a few TED talks yourself. It's not about copying other speakers or conforming to a cookie-cutter approach, it's about making sure you understand what you need to do to get your idea across in such a short amount of time in a way that will work for both a live and online audience.

You need to be relevant enough to your audience so that they can engage with your subject, but you need to be specific enough that it feels tangible and real to that audience. The mistake I see a lot of TEDx speakers making is that they go too broad. In trying to make something relevant, they pull the lens so far back that it becomes more and more abstract and they end up talking about nothing. The best advice I can give here is to repeat David Biello's thoughts on specificity (see 'Why should they care?' for more): 'My hypothesis, or my argument that I push people towards, is that specifics are actually the key to universality. So it's not so much that you and I have both been to the specific woods that I like to walk through in the Adirondacks that I'm going to include in my nature-based solutions, but you've walked through some woods, or you know what that is from reading books or whatever else. Weirdly, having those specific details of this was my experience as I was walking through the Adirondacks, I encountered this pine tree ... that seems like you're actually closing off universality. Actually you're opening it up, giving people hooks where they're like, *Oh yes, I too, have had an experience with a tree.*'

Ask yourself 'what is the change I'm making in my field?', or 'What is the specific thing I'm doing here that I want to share with others?', and *then* the task is to make that specific thing relevant to the wider world. When approaching a TEDx talk, I would recommend spending a lot of time in the 'planning' section of this book.

I truly believe that everyone has the capacity to give a great TEDx talk, but after more than a decade of experience curating TEDx events and coaching speakers, I've also realised that not every idea suits this format. Not every single idea suits a monologue of a maximum of eighteen minutes while standing on a red circle carpet, and that's okay.

And do not underestimate the importance of rehearsal, practice, or whatever you want to call it! I know there's a whole section in this book about how to prepare and how to internalise your content, but it's rarely more important to do that than when approaching a TED or TEDx talk, due to the fact they're filmed and have the potential to be seen by an audience of thousands or millions over time. Nancy Duarte, the public speaking expert who invented the Sparklines concept that I shared with you in the story structure section, said in a 2024 blog post that it took her eighteen hours to rehearse her most recent 18-minute talk – that's the equivalent of sixty full run-throughs. Many TED coaches I've worked with have said it takes sixty hours of work to give a great talk – from initial ideas to standing on stage. Given both the longevity and potential audience for a TEDx or TED talk, I would always advise taking the time commitment needed seriously.

You should hopefully be getting support from the curator of the TED or TEDx event that has booked you, and I really recommend working as much as you can with that person. Any opportunities they offer you to practise, learn, develop your talk, you should take them. I worked extensively with Payzee Mahmod on her TEDxLondonWomen talk, 'A survivor's plea to end child marriage', for example. 'You need people in your corner. You need people who know what they're doing. I had no idea the amount, the process, the work that goes into preparing for a TEDx. It's a whole process and you need to be open to that. You need to be open to learning and trusting the people that you work with,' she said. While I don't want you to be intimidated by the task at hand, I do want you to understand what an opportunity and a responsibility it is, and not to walk away from it feeling as if you could have done more!

If you'd like to know even more about prepping for a TEDx talk, may I recommend you read Chris Anderson's book, *TED Talks* (2016).

I've been asked to chair a panel and I'm nervous! How do I prepare?

Chairing a panel is a stealth kind of public speaking. This might be at a work conference or talking to an author at your local bookshop or a film festival. It doesn't necessarily require you to create a talk or presentation, but it absolutely does require some quite serious prep. Do not wing it! All of the advice I have for event chairs revolves around the same theme: respect and preparation. And the good news is that doing your due diligence in really small and manageable ways can add up to a radically different and positive experience for your panellists and your audience.

Let's start with an often-overlooked and really basic element of events like these. Take a look at the list of speakers and ask yourself if you've ever heard their names said aloud before, preferably by the person themselves. The answer might surprise you! When introducing your panel, you absolutely don't want to get off on the wrong foot by mispronouncing someone's name, especially if it's a name from a culture other than your own. And even if you think you know, it's always worth a cursory check: it's easy to get caught out by a Sara who pronounces it Sarah or a Charles who's actually

French. It's completely acceptable to ask everyone to say their name ahead of the event so you can introduce them properly. Better that than making a mistake! This also goes for people's pronouns, as you definitely don't want to start your panel by misgendering someone. I recommend you ask *everyone*, not just the panellists you think might be gender-non-conforming. This also goes for people's names, and you should ask everyone to say their name aloud for you, not just the people of colour or people you think might have 'complicated' names.

Bethany Rutter, who is an author and a seasoned chair of literary events, has one question she *always* asks panellists ahead of time. 'I don't think I've ever interviewed someone without asking if there's anything they don't want to talk about,' she told me. 'It might be something they've spoken about before, so you think it's fair game because you've been doing your prep and read interviews with them where they've talked about it, but maybe they've decided they've had enough. It could just be that they always get asked the same question and they're simply bored of answering it. Whatever the reason, it's good to know if anything is off-limits so you have time to pivot and write more questions, not to mention avoid creating an uncomfortable atmosphere for the audience and panellists.'

While we're talking about small but impactful pre-event preparation, may I recommend checking that everyone's bio is up to date? I can't tell you the number of times that organisers just copy and paste a bio from a random place on the internet and then chairs end up referencing a job someone did five years ago, rather than whatever they're working on right now. Ask your panel how they would like to be introduced, if there's any project in particular you should highlight in relation to the panel, and if anything's changed since the bio you've received.

A practical tip I would give for event chairs is that it looks *so much better* if you write your questions on a paper notebook rather than bringing them up on a note on your phone. There's just something so much more professional about someone holding a notebook and pen than having a phone in their hand, even if we know they're using it for legit reasons! Plus, when you jot interesting things or additional questions down while someone's talking, it doesn't look like you're ignoring them to play on your phone. It's about the optics, and whatever you can do to make your panel and the audience feel like they're in safe hands is worth doing.

I also recommend having *way* more questions than you need. You never know when a panellist is going to surprise you by being much more taciturn or fast-talking than you expected, rattling through what's meant to be a forty-five minute Q&A in half the time, leaving you needing to quickly pivot on the spot and come up with more questions. Equally, if someone's answers are just too short, it could be because they're conscious of not taking up too much time or talking over other panellists. If that's not something you're worried about, you can always prompt them to add more with gentle suggestions like 'that's really interesting, could you tell us a bit more about that?' or 'I'm actually not familiar with that idea, would you be able to elaborate?', which hopefully will signal that it's completely acceptable for the spotlight to stay on them.

It's valuable to be attuned to the possible dynamics of a panel (without projecting or making assumptions), and thinking about which of them might naturally be more dominant and talkative, and who might be holding back. Often, but not always, gender, race and class are at play here. I hope it's not too much of a shock for me to say that well-off white men are generally happy to speak at length, and often feel secure in their status as an expert. Making sure that all the panellists are given equal opportunity to speak may require some judicious handling by you as the chair.

As well as checking the pronouns of the people on your panel ahead of time, if you're chairing an event with audience questions included, it's important to be mindful of this when calling upon audience members. It's unnecessary to use gendered language when referring to people in the audience with their hands up, and could cause hurt or offence. Bethany told me she always describes people based on where they're sitting in the audience and what they're wearing. 'I always say something like *the person in the purple jacket near the front, and then I'll come to the red-haired person on the left*, and have never found that approach to fail!'

Since we're talking about Q&As – this can always be a bit tricky. I like to set out some ground rules at the start and play a bit of a 'bad cop' so that the panelists can feel more comfortable. The rules are quite simple: questions not comments, only one question per person and keep it short. I also like to take questions in pairs or three at a time – this way you let the panel focus on the questions they want to answer, it also lets you subtly reword any questions that don't quite make sense! Also, everyone doesn't have to answer everything – so feel free to direct questions to specific speakers. Finally, I always like to ask the last question myself - this way the panel can end with purpose rather than with a random question you can't predict in advance.

Much of this advice basically involves speaking to the people on the panel ahead of time, and this is something you could do weeks in advance or, if that's not possible, just asking for half an hour together before the event starts will go a long way. Make sure everyone involved is clear on the purpose of the event and why they have been invited.

The key, as always, is preparation, and whatever you can do to show you care, and are invested in the comfort of your panellists and audience, will go a long way. Also, a lot of this will help you prepare if you are asked to be on a panel, not just chairing it.

I've been asked to give a speech at a wedding! Help!

Being asked to give a speech at a wedding is a huge honour, but can feel like an overwhelming responsibility. I would argue this is one of the nicest kinds of public speaking: you're not asking your audience to change their mind, you're not delivering difficult information, you're not pitching for funding. You're just sharing memories about people they already know and love. Simon Bucknall is especially wise on the subject of wedding speeches (he's written more than one book on the subject), so a lot of what follows comes directly from his experience and knowledge.

Firstly: if you're feeling anxious, panicky and don't know where to start, do not go to ChatGPT and ask it to write you a best man speech! Instead, start by asking what the couple wants. This can include any topics that are off-limits for whatever reason (including cultural differences you might not have considered), and can help guide you in developing the content.

The two words that should be forefront in your mind when trying to put your wedding speech together are *focused* and *heartfelt*. This means no rambling, meandering speeches, and no amateur stand-up comedy.

I know, you've seen *hilarious* YouTube videos of a best man making an outrageous speech, but attempt to copy at your peril. Sure, making people laugh is always a nice feeling, but if you go in with *that* being your intention, it can end up feeling more like bad stand-up than a moment that centres the happy couple. You may be tempted to think of the most outrageous thing your friend has ever done, or reference the most niche inside joke you two have, but remembering your audience is just as important for a wedding speech as it is for any other kind of public speaking.

You don't want your audience feeling left out or just plain baffled, you want them to smile in recognition at your powers of observation. Make anecdotes real and make them personal to the couple. Think of the characteristics that make either of them who they are, then think of experiences or stories that illustrate that quality, and these can form the building blocks of your speech. These stories might end up being funny, but the focus should be on saying something true and heartfelt, which *could* also be humorous.

Oh, and keep it short: speeches often take place between courses at weddings, so the last thing you want is to embark on a twenty-minute magnum opus when your audience is only thinking about the chicken that's waiting in the wings once you're done. Close with something kind, warm and heartfelt that makes this speech feel like a gift to the couple.

Maryam Pasha

On the day, remember to breathe and speak slowly and clearly (especially if it's an international wedding where some guests may not have a perfect grasp of English), and try not to forget that the audience is on your side! They want you to give a good speech, and they love the newlyweds as much as you do. More than anything, try to enjoy it! You're forming an important part of a really special day. It's a privilege, not a burden.

How can I use public speaking and storytelling to be better at networking?

There are a lot of great insights about networking out there and I'd recommend seeking those out. In my opinion, the most fundamental part of being a better networker is curiosity. Be. More. Curious. Obviously this is something you can apply to all areas of your life and your life will get more interesting, but I think it's specifically wise to apply it to the idea of networking. This opinion is shared by Alana Drew, TEDxLondon's Head of People – someone who knows a thing or two about networking. And this doesn't just mean being curious about the specific thing you're interested in or want to talk about: it means being curious about the *people* you're engaging with. She says: 'I remember things about people. So someone might tell me their daughter is going to school for the first time. I will make a mental note to remember that, and I will naturally remember it, because I really care about those things. The next time I see that person, first and foremost it is, *How are you? How did day one of school go?* And that person immediately says, *Oh my gosh. How did you remember that?* Because it's important to me, because relationships are important, starting with those personal things then builds a bridge to getting into more of the other things with people.'

Even if you don't know someone well enough to have this kind of background information, asking questions is still the way to go. Approaching new people with curiosity is basically the same principle as doing background research on your audience: if I meet someone new, I often ask them if they do a lot of public speaking, do they go to a lot of events, because it's easier to frame what I do in that context. If they don't, I might ask them if they've heard of TED and find other ways to make connections between their world and mine. It can be very obvious when people go into these networking situations with a really clear goal (and remember, it's not necessarily a bad thing to approach an event with the goal to find someone to help you with a specific task or job), and that's often because they come across as false, or like they're not interested in hearing what other people have to say. By asking questions first, you can figure out a natural way in for the things you want to share without it feeling forced.

When networking, it's really important to remember that you're still talking to a real person. I think it's easy to get so wrapped up in your purpose that you can start to see people in these situations as a means to achieving your goals, but they're fully-formed humans too, with their own agendas and experiences. Alana told me about the EACH model, developed by Lucy Adams, who runs Disruptive HR. The theory is that every Employee is an Adult, a Consumer and a Human being, and while it's generally used to think about leadership, I think it's also relevant here when it comes to networking in general. How does thinking about a person through these three lenses change how you interact with them, if it changes anything at all?

Having a few relevant and interesting stories ready to go is always helpful. Anticipating what you might be asked, like 'what do you do?' or 'what brings you here' and having a story that answers those questions will make you stand out. It's more interesting for the person you're talking to and will feel more comfortable for you. And it's a great place to test out material – stories, anecdotes, analogies – that you can then use elsewhere!

Can I use storytelling when I'm trying to fundraise?

If you ask me, you absolutely can and should be using storytelling in your fundraising work. But don't just take my word for it: I talked about this question with Heidi Lindvall, who's a General Partner at a fund that invests in climate technology companies.

When I asked her about the role of storytelling in fundraising, her message was clear. 'Everything is storytelling. You're convincing people of a future that you want to be a part of creating, and you're convincing them that you're the best person to do that. That's storytelling.'

Heidi has extensive experience of working with company founders, and she loves encountering people who begin by telling their own story. 'I want to get to know the founders, and I want to know why they do what they do. What drives them? Where does their passion come from?' These kinds of questions are the absolute perfect opportunity to bring in all of your storytelling experience to paint a really vivid picture of *why* you're doing this work, first and foremost, before you even get to the point of asking for money. She told me that too many founders she meets enter these pitch meetings thinking that funds only care about the product and the technology, but getting to know the person and the story behind the product is key for her.

Heidi sees storytelling as a way of welcoming people in, rather than imposing on them. She sees a lot of founders who think their story is 'to convince people', which she sees as an 'outward action', whereas it should be about reversing that and bringing people in, encouraging them to become enthusiastic and energised by their story along with them.

The bottom line with fundraising? No one wants to be bored. There isn't some alternative standard of public speaking that we apply to fundraising and philanthropy. Your presentations should still be well structured and compelling, bringing in the principles of storytelling and speaking that you've learned throughout this book. Don't get it into your head that fundraising pitches need to be dry and didactic when something dynamic and memorable is more likely to get your audience where they need to be in order to fund your project.

Jennifer Kitt, who is an expert in fundraising, explained it so clearly. 'At some level, you want to create a moment where you're both almost like metaphorically sitting on the same side of the table, looking at the problem together. So it's an outcome orientation that somehow you're trying to get to, like curing cancer or investing in basic research so we can see the pathways for tomorrow, or helping green steel get past its barriers.' What would that moment look like for you and your audience? How do you create that sensation of you being on 'the same side of the table', rather than you on one side and them on the other? Story is always such a great way of helping someone to see what's at stake, and create that feeling of mutual understanding.

For me, the question is what stories do you need to tell for the person to look at the problem the way that you're looking at it, that will then allow you to explore *together* how money can play a role in this.

Something that goes a long way in fundraising is credibility. Although credibility is always important, when you're asking a person or an organisation to give you money, it's even more critical to do the work of establishing that you are a knowledgeable and trustworthy person. You'll be in a better position if you have been introduced to the room by someone who gives you credibility, maybe a member of staff or faculty that can back up your credentials. It's also completely acceptable to slightly modify your own story based on who you're speaking to. This doesn't mean to lie or embellish! It just means to amplify the bits of your experience that are more likely to resonate with them and help them to view you as credible. As Heidi puts it: 'If I'm speaking to a room of men who have been in venture capital for a long time, then I'll probably make a bigger point about the things I've done in the tech and start-up scene. If I'm speaking to people who aren't sure if they should take venture capital money, I tell them more about my documentary background and my Masters in human rights.'

I know it might sound obvious, but the foundation of fundraising is one very simple thing: money. We can be kind of weird and embarrassed when it comes to talking about money, but if your goal with your public speaking is to fundraise, you can't be ashamed of that goal. Nor should you be completely brazen about it either. You want to do the work with your talk or presentation so that you feel you've earned the opportunity to ask for the funds your project or organisation needs. Make sure you're well prepared and can respond to any questions the audience might have, or at least have a clear and confident answer on how you're going to get that information if you don't have it to hand.

What Now

How to use your time effectively (or my theory of quadrants)

At this point in my career, I've worked with speakers who are preparing for a whole range of different public speaking opportunities. Some of them are starting to work on their talk months out from the event, and others are coming to me in a real time crunch.

Obviously, more time is always better than less time, but sometimes there's just nothing you can do about it and you've got to work with what you have. Being really short on time doesn't mean you should skip the rehearsal or preparation step altogether and decide to wing it, it just means you need to focus your energy and attention in a particular way. That's why I've developed an approach to preparation that

	low importance	high importance
high time	**Practise and Test**	**5 Planning Steps + Script**
low time	**5 Planning Steps**	**5 Planning Steps + Outline**

corresponds to two specific factors, and I visualise it as quadrants.

This graphic is as low-tech as I can possibly make it, so let me break it down for you and give you more information!

I arrange preparation according to the level of importance of the event, and the amount of time that the speaker has to prepare for it. One way to think about the idea of importance can be to think about risk: is this a high-risk situation with a lot riding on it? Or is it low-risk without much impact? Obviously what's important to me and what's important to you are likely to be completely different based on your own circumstances.

Esha Bhandari, the US civil liberties lawyer I've referenced before in this book, expressed it to me like this: 'If I'm speaking to a bunch of legislators, that's high importance. I'm going to have to put more time into preparation. If I'm speaking to a group of supporters, and it's a low-pressure environment, I can try out ideas and points. I can even ask for feedback after to ask, *did you guys find this stuff persuasive?* You're definitely not arguing before the US Supreme Court every day. Those high importance things come very infrequently.'

High importance–high time

Getting the opportunity to speak about something important to you *and* having a lot of time to prepare for it? The dream. In situations like this, I would recommend writing yourself a script that you then find a way to internalise and also dedicating serious time to practising and getting feedback. This quadrant is basically where you take every step that I've broken down for you in this book and make time for all of it. In high importance–high time situations, you will never catch me using untested materials.

For example, if I was giving a TED talk or a workshop to a high-value client, I wouldn't use an analogy or a story that I haven't already road tested somewhere else to check that it works, to make sure that I know how to tell it, to make sure I'm emphasising the right parts so it makes sense, and to make sure it lands with the audience. I'd use the time leading up to the event to assure myself of that in as many situations as possible.

This is the best case scenario so make the most of it!

High importance–low time

. . . and in some ways we could argue this is the worst case scenario: you've been asked to speak, it's important but you have almost no time to prepare. How do you go about it, then? In my experience, the best approach is to go through the five steps I outline in the Planning section of this book:

1. What is your one core message?
2. Who is your audience?

3. How are you going to keep them listening?
4. What is the essential information you have to include?
5. What is your unique point of view?

As well as going through this list, I would strongly advocate for writing yourself an outline. While this doesn't mean a full script, because we don't have time for that, it means having a really clear grasp of all your key points in the order you want to hit them. Staying calm and trying to keep control of your material is key when it's high importance–low time. Making sure you've got a comprehensive account of everything you want to include, all the most important facts and figures and stories, and that you've got a simple structure that you can stick to, will be so helpful in a time-poor situation.

Now, on to the low importance quadrants. If ever you're approached to speak and it's something you deem of low importance, this is an amazing opportunity to hone the skills you'll need for the occasions that are of high importance. Don't just turn these opportunities down because they're not going to change your life, instead see them as part of the overall work.

Low importance–high time

Occasions that fall into low importance–high time are the *perfect* opportunity for you to practise. Practise what? Anything. Whatever element of public speaking or storytelling that you're not feeling totally on top of. Whenever you're speaking at work, whenever you're speaking with friends, if you have a new neighbour and decide to go round and introduce yourself, use that as an opportunity to test the things you want to say.

Back to the 'talking at your kid's school' example: use that as an opportunity to get really good at thinking about the five questions. Get familiar with what that process looks like, and get comfortable so that, when you have to give a talk or a presentation that feels more high-stakes to you, you've got the muscle memory from doing it on something that isn't totally mission-critical. Say you're going for coffee with a friend. Use that as a moment to ask yourself, what am I going to talk to them about today? What is the most important thing I want us to discuss? What are they going through right now that I might want to be mindful of or ask about? Do I have any stories I want to tell them? Those are all things that correspond to the big questions you need to address when planning any kind of public speaking, even if they don't seem like it.

They mean you're thinking about your audience, making sure you include the most important information, and giving yourself the opportunity to tell stories. Use this time to become more intuitive with how you approach the five questions so that it becomes a part of how you approach more scenarios than just public speaking.

Low importance–low time

Now, say that you're giving a talk at your kid's school this evening. That would mean it falls into the 'low importance' and 'low time' quadrant. When you're really pressed for time on something that isn't fundamentally that important, where you're not going to be squandering an opportunity to change the world but you still want to do a good job of the task at hand, I would recommend you focus solely on the five steps/questions listed previously. I see these as the inescapable part of any public speaking engagement, no matter how low-priority it is for you. As long as you at least spend a little time thinking about these five things, you should be in a good position to speak stress-free, and not put yourself in a situation where it looks obvious to your audience that you consider it 'low importance'.

Why we need your voice

In Isaac Asimov's science-fiction series *Foundation*, every time humanity faces a crisis a wise prophet emerges in holographic form to guide us through it. Sadly, there is no prophet waiting to save us from the converging crises we face today: climate change, the rise of uncontrolled AI, and the re-emergence of fascism. We are certainly not going to find a way through this mess by relying on old ideas. If anything is going to save us, it is new stories – and the new storytellers who will tell them.

In 2016 President Barack Obama said, while visiting Berlin, 'It's easier to make negative attacks and simplistic slogans than it is to communicate complex policies.' It's now a decade later and he is more right than ever.

It can sometimes seem that divisive and negative messages of fear and hate are more easily communicated. This can be seen all around us – the ongoing denial of climate change, anti-migrant sentiment, demonisation of poverty etc. These hateful messages are wrapped up with their own simplistic but effective stories, which is why they have spread so quickly. Yet, in reality, these are all complex problems that people spend years trying to understand, and the answers they come up with aren't automatically expressed in simple messages.

Ideas that can benefit the world are often difficult to present in ways that are clear for everyone to understand. Nuanced, clever solutions are often presented in inaccessible papers or talks that only appeal to our logic and not to our emotions.

This is where storytelling comes in; where the art of effective communication is essential. If more voices – both in number and in diversity – can translate these solutions into human stories, and fill our public and private spaces with clear and simple messages then there is a real chance to change the path we are all on. I've seen this first hand working with speakers like Payzee Mahmod, who took her own lived experience and told it to policy makers in a way they couldn't ignore. The result? England and Wales now have the most progressive and protective anti-child marriage legislation anywhere in the world. I've seen climate scientists, activists and policy makers – who, despite the headlines, are making progress – do this too. Is it fast or easy or inevitable – no. But is it possible? Yes.

Working with speakers and being trusted with their stories is a privilege that I don't take lightly. A client once observed that 'when you work with Maryam, you find out who you are, not just what to say.' This is a vulnerable process, and often you have to confront your gremlins before you can find your story and embrace your authenticity. My hope is that by reading this book you find the practical tools and support you need to develop your skills. My goal for you is to be a little better every day, so that when you look back years from now you can see the distance you've travelled and feel proud of the effort you put in.

Deep down, I want you to know, in your heart, something that I already know is true. Your voice is powerful, it is needed, and you can develop the skills for it to be heard.

Thank you for taking the time to read this book. Speak soon!

Further Resources

Watch

Ash Beckham: We're all hiding something
Ben Hurst: Boys won't be boys. Boys will be what we teach them to be
BLACK: My journey to yo-yo mastery
Chimamanda Ngozi Adichie: The danger of a single story
Clover Hogan: What to do when climate change feels unstoppable
Dan Gilbert: The psychology of your future self
Daniel Susskind: 3 myths about the future of work (and why they're not true)
Donnel Baird: Why you should ditch deadly fossil-fuel appliances
Fenhinti Balogun: How to find your voice for climate action
Galina Angarova: The hidden cost of the green transition's mineral rush
Hal Harvey and John Doerr: How to decarbonize the grid and electrify everything
Hamdi Ulukaya: The Anti-CEO Playbook
Jodie Jackson: Beyond fake news: how to heal a broken worldview
Jonathan Foley: The climate solutions worth funding – now

Kathryn A. Whitehead: The tiny balls of fat that could revolutionize medicine
Kris De Meyer: Feeling stuck on climate change? Here's what to do
Leigh Caldwell: The formula for privilege
Margaret Heffernan: Forget the pecking order at work
Melinda Janki: How we took on an oil giant—and won
Nancy Duarte: The secret structure of great talks
Nathalie McDermott: Why stories of trauma don't create change
Neil Vora: How to stop the pandemic? Stop deforestation
Origin (2023), directed by Ava DuVernay
Pattie Gonia: Why joy is a serious way to take action
Payzee Mahmod: A survivor's plea to end child marriage
Rachel Botsman: The currency of the new economy is trust
Roman Krznaric: How to be a good ancestor
Roman Krznaric: Lessons from history for a better future
Sahar Zand: Why Iranians are cutting their hair for "Woman, Life, Freedom"
Sathya Raghu Mokkapati Greenhouse-in-a-box: Affordable Climate Tech
Simon Bucknall: Why public speaking should be taught in schools
Sofie Hagen: You can be fat and happy
Sophie Morgan: Air travel is failing disabled people – here's the truth
Sophie Williams: The rigged test of leadership
Stefanie Reid: Why accessible design is for everyone

Stella Young: I'm not your inspiration, thank you very much

Vidhya Ramalingam: The real-world danger of online myths

Zak Ebrahim: I am the son of a terrorist. Here's how I chose peace

Read

TED TALKS: The Official Guide to Public speaking by Chris Anderson

Caste: The Origins of Our Discontents by Isabel Wilkerson

The Psychology of Curiosity: A Review and Reinterpretation by George Loewenstein

Listen

Speechless Podcast, Simon Bucknall and Maryam Pasha

Screw this . . . Let's try something else Podcast, Matt Golding and Maryam Pasha

Acknowledgements

There are many people without whom this book would not exist.

Let me start with Bethany Rutter, my writing partner and friend of nearly twenty years, who made this book possible in the most literal sense. Working with Bethany meant I got to spend time talking about something I love – stories – with someone I love, which made the entire experience a pleasure. Thank you for understanding the heart of this book immediately and capturing my voice with such skill and intuition. Your talent is extraordinary, and I am immensely grateful.

To everyone who generously agreed to be interviewed for this book: thank you for sharing your stories, insights, and time. Your voices are the heart of these pages, and this book is richer for your contributions.

Special shout out to Helen Tupper and Sarah Ellis, who told me I had to write this book in the first place – their conviction planted the seed; Sophie Williams and Julia Shaw helped me navigate the often bewildering world of publishing with wisdom and generosity; Sofie Hagen, Deesha Chandra and the whole TEDxLondon team, who cheered me on from the very beginning; Rebecca Menzies, who helped me imagine what this book could look like; and Rebecca Shellim, who kept everything on track.

Thank you to my agent Rachel Mills for your belief in me and your guidance and to Anna Steadman and the entire team at Headline Home for literally bringing this book to life.

And, finally, my husband, Leigh, who believed I could write this book long before I could even imagine it myself. Thank you for being the best collaborator and most loving person I know.

Index

'A survivor's plea to end child marriage' (Mahmod) 142–3
abundance mindset 24
accents 6, 165
accessibility 52
accuracy 162–3
acting 164
action 42–3
  call to 141–3
ad libs 67
Adams, Kenn 117
Adams, Lucy 255–6
Adichie, Chimamanda Ngozi 130
adrenaline 222–3
advocacy 227–30
Amplification 75–7, 127
analogies 55, 135–9
Anderson, Chris 25, 198, 245
Angarova, Galina 148
'The Anti-CEO Playbook' (Ulukaya) 79–80
anxiety 4
Asimov, Isaac 269
assembly 9, 12, 13–14, 15, 69, 72
assumptions, challenging 75
attention span 68, 73
audience 7, 15, 20, 171
  adapting to 38–40, 228–9
  attention span 68
  bridging gap with 160
  business settings 218
  care 41–8
  change of perspective 75–7
  connection points 36–7
  connection with 34
  and content structure 36–8
  danger of neglecting 31
  engagement 35
  feedback 32–3, 36
  fight-or-flight response 233
  knowledge 35
  listening to 32–3
  message alignment 32
  most difficult 39
  motivation 35–6, 43–5
  online speaking 215–16
  pitching level 51
  points of relevance 34
  response 25, 28
  size 4
  thinking about 31–5, 48, 59
  understanding 42, 267
  understanding feedback 196
  and visuals 187–8, 189
audience take aways 30
authentic self 159–60, 165, 199
authenticity 10, 159–60, 160–3, 163–4, 199, 270
authorities 5
authority 58, 64, 74, 89–90, 135
awareness raising 55

Baird, Donnel 147
Balogun, Fenhinti 93
Beckham, Ash 82
beginning and opening techniques. *see* opening and opening techniques
being yourself 56, 58–9

beliefs 43
Bergdorf, Munroe 158
Bhandari, Esha 25–6, 72, 205–6, 226, 264
Biello, David 46, 100–1, 229–30, 242–3
big idea 242
    avoid inspiring 27–9
    constituent parts 53–4
    developing 28
    the focus 24–5
    focus on 25–7, 30
    identifying 22–4, 26–7
    preparation work 26
BLACK 110–11
body language 156, 166–8
Botsman, Rachel 90, 145
brain, the 63
brain-teasing 87–8
breathing exercises 207
Brown, Brené 222
Bucknall, Simon 50, 71, 94, 169–70, 184–5, 213, 216, 251
business development 66
business settings 217–21
    audience 218
    storytelling 218–20
    templates 220–1

Caldwell, Leigh 99, 217–21, 219
Call To Action 127, 141–3
Callback, close 148–9
Campbell, Joseph 109, 110
care 41–8
case studies 49
cause and effect 219
cause-and-effect learning 99–100
challenge, culture of 38
change 105, 118, 140, 243, 270
    and storytelling 64–5, 67, 110, 113, 231–6
ChatGPT 251
Clance, Pauline Rose 202, 205
clichés 137
clickbait 44
climate change advocacy 227–30
closing 140
    Call To Action 141–3
    Callback 148–9
    on a high 140
    Reframe with a twist 150–1
    Take A Stand (with me) 144–5
    Zoom Out 146–7
clothes 156, 171, 172, 173–5
code-switching 161–2
cognitive load 171, 173
combative situations 38
comedians 184–5
communication 195
communication style 5–6
    adapting 39
communicators 158
comparisons 210
complex issues 227–30
confidence 3, 7–8, 45, 57, 156, 180, 208
    building 8
    and clothes 174
    feigning 3
    loss of 8–9
    and material mastery 163–5
    and practice 181
conflict 110–11, 112, 114–16
connection 34
consequences, focus on 118–19
content 15
    choice 45
    compelling 45
    editorial decisions 22
    importance 157
    tailoring 45–7
control 15
Converging Ideas story structure 101, 132–3
conversational circles 23
Coren, Emily 64–5
Countdown 4
creative storytellers 79
credibility 35, 106, 259
cultural expectations 5
cultural references 136
curiosity 44–5, 47, 75, 87–8, 97, 254–5
curiosity-provoking 28
'The currency of the new economy is trust' (Botsman) 90–1

De Meyer, Kris 28, 42–3, 64–5
decision making 39–40, 45, 46–7
delivery 9, 12, 14, 15, 157
   authenticity 159–60, 160–3, 163–4
   body language 156, 166–8
   clothes 171, 172, 173–5
   confidence 163–5
   experience of 166
   eye contact 168–9
   importance 155–7
   mastery of material 163–5
   questions 170–1
   sitting 172–3
   standing 172–3
   style 158
   voice 156, 158–65
   volume 169–70
disclaimers 74
discrimination, structural 6–7
dislikeability, facing 58
distractions 73, 74
diving in 19
Doerr, John 102–3
doubts 201, 205
drag 174–5
dramatic effect 87–8
Drew, Alana 8–9, 254, 255
Duarte, Nancy 65, 126–8, 244
DuVernay, Ava 133

EACH model 255–6
Ebrahim, Zak 124, 125
editing 22, 24, 52
effectiveness 31–2
Ellis, Sarah 32–3, 224–5
emotional connections 14
emotional response 25
emotions 28, 56–7, 67, 81–3, 106, 237–8
empathy 65, 232
empowerment 223–4
end, choice 151
engagement 35, 195
enthusiasm 47, 56–7, 215
Environmental Research Letters 64–5
essential information 20

evidence-based optimism 106–7
examples 196
expectations, re-setting 85
experience, using 46
experiences, unique 55
experts 158, 160–1, 182
eye contact 168–9, 214

fake it til you make it 3, 45, 208–10
False Start openings 84–6
fears 4
feedback 156, 164, 183, 193–200, 214, 225
   audience 32–3, 36
   on audience understanding 196
   on communication 195
   on examples 196
   on flow 197
   on good points 198–9
   on jargon 197
   on level 198
   on opening 195
   perspective 199
   questions 195–9
   on re-engagement points 198
   using 199–200
feelings 25
feminist discourse 5–6
FFT 222
fight-or-flight response 233
first impressions 73
Fisher, Rebecca 68, 163–5, 174
flashbacks 123–5
flexibility 180
flexible thinking 85–6
flow 65, 178, 179, 197
focus 10, 20, 24–5, 30, 228
Foley, Jonathan 162–3, 229
foundations, laying 20
frustration 15
fundraising 257–60

gatekeeping 160–1
gaze 168–9
general public, the 39
gentleness 5–6
Gilbert, Dan 46–7

Goldberg, Briar 31–2, 163–4, 176–7, 179, 180, 182
Golding, Matt 43, 112–13
Gonia, Pattie 25, 175, 199
'Greenhouse- in-a-Box: Affordable Climate Tech' (Mokkapati) 76–7
group scenarios, story structures for 131–3

habits 167–8
hackneyed phrases 137
Hagen, Sofie 65, 71, 148–9, 168–9, 185, 194
Haidt, Jonathan 63
Hajim, Corey 29, 189, 197, 223
Harvey, Hal 102–3
Heffernan, Margaret 70, 93–4
The Heroine's Journey story structure 112–13
The Hero's Journey story structure 65, 109–11, 112, 117
'The hidden cost of the green transition's mineral rush' (Angarova) 148–9
high importance preparation 263, 264, 264–6
high-level ideas, translating 135
Hogan, Clover 38–9, 43, 193–4, 227, 228
hooks 47, 87–8
'How to decarbonize the grid and electrify everything' (Harvey and Doerr) 102–3
'How we took on an oil giant—and won' talk (Janki) 121–2
Hudson, Kim 113
human-centred approach 231–6
humour 95
Hurst, Ben 34, 161–2, 181, 215, 238

'I am the son of a terrorist. Here's how I chose peace' (Ebrahim) 124, 125
ideas 241–2
    exploratory phase 23
    generating 15
    high-level 135
    making comprehensible 135–9
    too many 22

identity, marginalised 4–5
identity statements 223–4
imagery 94
Imes, Suzanne 202, 205
impact, long term 238–9
impact storytelling 231–6
impostor syndrome 5, 156, 157, 201
    author's experience 202–5
    origins of 202–6
    overcoming 206–10
In Medias Res story structure 65, 123–5
inauthenticity 163–4
information, essential 20
information deficit model 229–30
information gap 44, 97
insecurity 3, 5
inspiring, avoiding 27–9
internalisation 156, 176, 179–83, 265
investment, pitching for 218
invisibility 2

Jackson, Jodie 36–7, 67, 208–9, 223–4
Janki, Melinda 121–2
jargon 162–3, 197
Jobs, Steve 126, 127, 158

keep it simple 50–3
key points 49–54
King, Martin Luther Jr 126, 127
Kishotenketsu story structure 114–16
Kitt, Jennifer 167–8, 258–9
Kondo, Marie 134
Krznaric, Roman 132, 172–3, 191, 216, 234

language 34–5, 136, 137, 229
learning 97
life experience, using 94, 238–40
Lindvall, Heidi 257–8, 259
listening, to audience 32–3
lived experiences, sharing 94, 238–40
Loewenstein, George 44–5, 97
longer-form content 101, 119–20, 129–30
low importance preparation 263, 266–8

McCaffrey, Mark 64–5
McDermott, Nathalie 55, 231–3
Mahmod, Payzee 70, 142–3, 233, 238–40, 244, 270
manga comics 115
marketing 30
material, mastery of 163–5
media output 55
memorisation 177, 179–80
mentors 194
message 22, 242
  accurate 162–3
  audience alignment 32
  identifying 20
  keep it simple 50–3
  and questions 91
  story structures and 102
  tailoring 42
metaphors 135–9, 229
microphones 73, 170, 171
mindset 73
misdirection 84
mission, focus on 30
Mokkapati, Sathya Raghu 76–7
monomyth 109
Morgan, Sophie 81–2
motivation, audience 35–8, 43–5
The Mountain Range story structure 101, 120–2
Muir, William 70
Mullender, Richard 92
Murdock, Maureen 113
muscle memory 267
'My journey to yo-yo mastery' (BLACK) 110–11
My Neighbour Totoro (film) 115

Naidoo, Kumi 52, 54–5, 225–6
narrative 50
  building 119
  elements 25
  layering 129–30
Narrative openings 93–5
natural speakers 1
negative messages 269–70
nerves 207, 208–9
overcoming 222–6
Nested Loops story structure 101, 129–30
networking 254–6

Obama, Barack 269
objective 105
Ocasio-Cortez, Alexandria 158
Odyssey (Homer) 65
off the cuff 184–6
older white men 5
one-to-one conversations 32
online speaking 213–16
openings and opening techniques 73–4
  Amplification 75–7
  choosing 96–8
  feedback on 195
  False Start 84–6
  Narrative 93–5
  Personalisation 81–3
  Puzzle 87–8
  Question 89–92
  Sensory 78–80
optimism, evidence-based 106–7
outlines 176, 266
overwhelm 8–9, 36

panels
  audience questions 249–50
  bios 247–8
  chairing 246–50
  dynamics 249
  introductions 246–7
  notebooks 248
  off-limits topics 247
  questions 248–50
paradoxes 88
Parasite (film) 115
Parker, Trey 100
Pasha, Maryam
  background 1–5, 119
  and impostor syndrome 202–5
passion 45, 47, 56–7, 232–3
Perry, Philippa 88
personal commitment 144–5
personal information 56, 58–9, 69–70

personal storytelling 233, 237–40
personalisation 81–3, 90–1, 106
perspective 80
  keeping 226
  unique 20, 23, 55–6
persuasion moments 180
Petals story structure 101, 131–2
phases 9, 12–15
pitching level 51
Pixar Pitch story structure 65, 101, 117–19
place, sense of 78–9
planning 9, 12, 13, 15
  diving in 19
  importance 19–21
  online speaking 216
  stages 20–1
practice 181–6, 224, 243–4
preamble 74
predictable, the, disrupting 84
preparation 26, 156, 224
  high importance 263, 264, 264–6
  low importance 263, 266–8
  panel chairing 246–50
  TEDx talks 241–5
  time management 263–8
private information 56, 58–9
Problem-Solution story structure 101, 105–8, 220
professionals 160–1
psychological connections 14
psychology, retraining 208–9
'The psychology of your future self' (Gilbert) 46–7
purpose 151
  clarity of 233
  identifying 20
  sense of 228
  speaking with 4
Puzzle openings 87–8
puzzles 87–8

questions 29–30, 36, 117–18
  asking 170–1
  closed 89
  feedback 195–9
  knowledge-based 89–90
  and message 91
  and networking 254–5
  open 89
  opening 89–92
  panels 248–50
  personalisation 90–1
  rhetorical 90

Ramalingam, Vidhya 34–5, 66, 106–7, 224
real self, showing 56, 58–9
re-engagement points 198
Reframe with a twist close 150–1
rehearsing 156, 177, 181–6, 224, 243–4
Reid, Stefanie 84–5
relevance 20, 35, 242–3
reprogramming 208–9
research findings 125
rewiring 208–9
role 68
Rutter, Bethany 247, 249–50

Sagan, Carl 229
sales, and storytelling 66
Sasson, Sivan 166, 167, 186
scale, change of 75–7, 146–7
scarcity mindset 24
schema 217–18
scientific communication 229
scripting 156
scripts and scripting 67, 176–9, 265
  benefits 177–8
  downsides 178–9
  internalisation 176, 179–83
  memorisation 177, 179–80
  mental 178
  outlines 176, 266
  rehearsing 177, 181–6
'The secret structure of great talks' (Duarte) 126–8
self
  authentic 159–60, 165, 199
  sense of 228
sense-making 65
Sensory openings 78–80

set up, questions about 170–1
sexism 205
shoes 174–5
signposting 74
simple but effective mantra 4
single overriding communication objective (SOCO) 25, 32
skills, building 3–4, 14
Slean, Cheryl 64–5
slides 187–92
   audience and 187–8, 189
   colour scheme 190
   as a preparation tool 191
   presentation deck 191
   role 188–9, 189, 192
   simplicity 189–90
   spell-checking 191
   style 190
   template 190
   text 187
social media 27
SOCO (single overriding communication objective) 25, 32
solutions, offering 233–4
Sparklines story structure 65, 101, 126–8
specifics and specificity 46, 146, 242–3
speeches 251–3
statistics 49, 51, 54
Stone, Matt 100
stories 54–5
   choice 103
   conceptualisation 67
   sources 71–2
Story Sandwich story structure 101, 102–4
story structures 63, 65–7, 99–100
   beats 100, 109
   building 119
   built in endings 140
   choice 111, 134
   Converging Ideas 101, 132–3
   flashbacks 123–5
   for group scenarios 131–3
   The Heroine's Journey 112–13
   The Hero's Journey 65, 109–11, 112, 117
   key to 103
   Kishotenketsu 114–16
   longer-form content 101, 120–1, 129–30
   In Medias Res 65, 123–5
   message and 102
   The Mountain Range 101, 120–2
   Nested Loops 101, 129–30
   Petals 101, 131–2
   Pixar Pitch 65, 101, 117–19
   Problem-Solution 101, 105–8, 220
   Sparklines 101, 126–8
   story led 100–1
   Story Sandwich 101, 102–4
   using 99
storytelling 3–4, 10, 14, 15, 99
   beginning. *see* openings and opening techniques
   benefits 67, 67–9
   in business settings 218–20
   and change 64–5, 67, 110, 113, 231–6
   control 237
   effectiveness 63–5
   flow 65
   and fundraising 257–60
   good 99–100
   impact 231–6
   importance 100–1
   long term impact 238–9
   and networking 254–6
   personal 69–70, 233
   role 64, 270
   and sales 66
   skill development 70–1
   sources 71–2, 94
structural discrimination 6–7
structural factors 4–5
structure 15
style 157, 158
subversion 84
support 239–40, 244–5
surprise, sense of 76
Susskind, Daniel 150–1

Take A Stand (with me) close 144–5
technical issues 171

TED Talks (Anderson) 245
TEDx talks, preparation 241–5
TEDxEastEnd 3
TEDxLondon 4
theme 23, 25
think, feel, do framework 25
'3 myths about the future of work (and why they're not true)' (Susskind) 150–1
throughlines 25
Thunberg, Greta 158
time limits 180, 183–4
time management 263–8
'The tiny balls of fat that could revolutionize medicine' 138–9
titles 29–30
tone 136, 178–9
traumatic experiences, sharing 238–40
Trojan Horse approach 174–5, 228
Tupper, Helen 32–3, 63–4

Ulukaya, Hamdi 79–80
unexpected, the 180
unique perspective 20, 23, 55–6
universality and universalisation 46, 82

visuals 156, 187–92
    audience and 187–8, 189
    colour scheme 190
    as a preparation tool 191
    presentation deck 191
    role 188–9, 189, 192
    simplicity 189–90
    spell-checking 191
    style 190
    template 190
Vogler, Christopher 109, 110
voice 156
    authentic 6, 159–60, 164–5
    finding 2, 158–65
    volume 169–70
voiceless, feeling 5–6
volume 169–70
Vora, Neil 24–5, 32, 199–200

W, the 168–9
wedding speeches 251–3
'We've stopped trusting institutions and started trusting strangers' (Botsman) 145
Whitehead, Kathryn A. 138–9
'Why accessible design is for everyone' (Reid) 84–5
'Why Iranians are cutting their hair for "Woman, Life, Freedom"' (Zand) 89–90
'Why you should ditch deadly fossil fuel appliances' (Baird) 147
Wilkerson, Isabel 133
Williams, Sophie 58, 68, 235–6

yonkoma 116
'You can be fat and happy' (Hagen) 148
Young, Stella 81–2

Zand, Sahar 89–90
Zoom Out close 146–7